Early Elementary K-3 Book One
An Introduction to the Visual Arts

Written by Brenda Ellis
Edited by Ariel DeWitt and Daniel D. Ellis
Cover, book design and illustrations by Brenda Ellis
Students' works were created in art classes Mrs. Ellis taught from 1992-2008.

Third Edition

ACKNOWLEDGMENTS

Thanks to all the students who participated in the lessons and to those who let us share their work with others through this book. Thanks to Christine Ann Feorino and Iris De Long for editing the first edition of this book. Thanks to Dover Publications Inc., NY and Art Resources, NY for supplying the fine art images by the great masters.

Printed in the U.S. A.
ISBN 978-1-939394-01-9

Published by
Artistic Pursuits Inc.
Northglenn, Colorado
www.artisticpursuits.com
alltheanswers@artisticpursuits.com

THE Curriculum for Creativity ™

ARTistic Pursuits®

EARLY ELEMENTARY K-3
BOOK ONE

An Introduction to the Visual Arts

A Comprehensive Art Program Designed to Involve the Student in the Creative Process While Developing Observational Skills

Newly Expanded and Revised

Art Instruction
PLUS Master Works Including Ancient Art

36 Lessons with Projects

Brenda Ellis

Contents

Page   Lesson

Materials

Materials needed for this book are listed in groups. Each project is given a material group number so that you will know what you need to complete the project by referring to this page. Having these items on hand will make the preparation for each art class simple.

GROUP #1 DRAWING

1- Ebony pencil
1 - Vinyl eraser
1 - Small set of soft pastels
(Powdery like chalk, not professional grade)
1 - Small set of oil pastels
(*CrayPas, Junior Artist* brand recommended)
1 - Sketch or drawing paper pad

GROUP #2 PAINTING

1 – Set of 10-15 Watercolor Crayons (*Caran d'ache, Neocolor II Watersoluble* brand recommended)
1 - #8 round watercolor brush that comes to a point.
1 - Watercolor paper pad

GROUP #3 PAPER ART

1 -heavy weight construction paper, assorted colors including black
1 -package tissue paper, assorted colors
1 -scissors (Fiskars for children are recommended.)

GROUP #4 CLAY

1 -4 or 5 lb. gray self hardening clay
(Red self-hardening clay can be substituted and may be preferred for the Greek pot project in lesson 28. White self-hardening clay or a flour dough recipe can be used in lesson 23.)

Group #1
Additional items: cotton cloth and masking tape in lesson 33, brown wrapping paper in lesson 22, white roll of paper in lesson 25. Group #1 is used in lessons 3, 6, 8, 9, 10, 14, 17, 19, 20, 21, 22, 25, 26, and 29.

Group # 2
Additional items: Paper towels, empty cans for water containers, and a pencil. Group #2 is used in lessons 1, 4, 5, 6, 7, 11, 12, 13, 18, 24, and 35.

Group #3
Additional items: glue stick, pencil, string, and ruler. Group #3 is used in lessons 15, 16, 28, 32, 34, and 36.

Group # 4
Additional items: rolling pin, 4 inch paper tube, and foil. Group #4 is used in lessons 23, 27 28, 30, and 31. Option: substitute lesson 23 with a flour dough recipe.

Teaching Simply

This book is designed to involve each child in a time of parent/child interaction followed by a time of working independently. Parents read the lesson, participate with the child in short observation activities or discuss art works by the masters, and then provide the child with materials for the art project. The child creates original works of art about subjects of his or her choosing. This book can be used at home or in the classroom.* Lessons take five to ten minutes to present. Optional exercises will take longer. Projects take thirty to sixty minutes, depending on the child's approach and attention span.

WHAT ARTISTS DO

The first section of the book covers the activities artists engage in when making art (composing, imagining, looking), how to use the materials of an artist (watercolor crayons, pastels, pencil), and the various types of subjects artists work from (landscapes, people, still life). Activities broaden the child's awareness of the world he or she lives in. The child explores drawing and painting in this section. Fourteen lessons give students plenty of opportunities to find out just what it is to be an artist!

WHAT ARTISTS SEE

The second section of the book covers the elements that artists use in two-dimensional and three-dimensional work such as shape, form, line, and color. The child explores collage, paper works, drawing and color mixing while gaining experience in handling scissors, glue, folding paper forms, drawing materials, and using a brush. Seven lessons give children opportunities to make art that originates from their interests.

WHERE WE FIND ART

The third section of the book looks at art in caves, pyramids, cathedrals, etc., covering ancient art from cave paintings to book illumination of the Middle Ages. The child uses various media including chalk pastels, oil pastels, clay, and paper works. The child explores mural, pottery, clay modeling, paper art, bookbinding, and mosaic techniques. Fifteen lessons give children even more opportunities to explore art media while learning about the many places in which ancient cultures created art.

*Since classroom environments are often more limited than the home, the teacher in a classroom will need to bring in interesting subjects for children to work from and observe. Pots, models, a jar of goldfish, a shell collection, or bowls of fruit and vegetables are just some of the rich sources I've found at home or have been able to purchase for a small price. Small caged pets such as lizards, turtles, rabbits, etc. can be brought in by students who own them and create high student interest. Suggested outings can be local, and I highly encourage you to take them! Simply stepping outdoors provides an active, rich environment from which children can create.

Artists Compose

Lesson 1

Artists place things together to create something new. They compose. Musicians place notes together to make songs that we hear. Choreographers put body movements together to make dances that we feel. In theatre, story and song are put together to make plays that we act out. Visual artists place images together to make pictures that we see.

Music, dance, theatre, and visual arts are all part of what we call the ARTS. This book is about visual artists. They work with the way things look. They put things together in new ways so others can see a part of the world the way the artist sees or imagines it. Artists move objects and colors around, composing their pictures, so that we can see the subjects in new ways.

I've Done That! Exercise

Talk about the things you have done in the arts. They may be things like playing a musical instrument, singing, dancing, participating in a play, drawing a picture, or modeling sand or play dough.
Note: Create awareness of the arts by discussing areas in which the student has already participated.
Participation does not mean to have performed the piece in front of others. Simply doing any of these things helps in understanding the arts and feeling comfortable with having already done it.

This lesson teaches us that artists compose things we hear, feel, act, and see. This book is about artists who put together things that we see.

Look at Composition
In 17th Century Netherlands

The artist composed this painting to show two views at the same time. On the right, a woman in a blue skirt and two men casually talk while the men relax. On the left, a child in a yellow skirt sits in an open doorway. The artist framed each view in special ways so that we notice the figures. The group is surrounded by a bower constructed with trellis-work. This dark wood catches our attention. The girl is framed by the arched doorway with red brick pattern. Her white cap stands out from the dark interior behind it.

A girl with a yellow skirt sits in the closest doorway. What does she hold?

How many doorways do you look through in this painting?

What hangs on the red window shutter?

Pieter De Hooch's early paintings show life as it was lived around the home. What do you think the barrel and the pot might be used for? Which one could hold water for washing floors or clothing?

What part of the painting tells us that this is a clear, sunny day?

Pieter De Hooch, *The Courtyard of a House in Delft*, 1658.
Photo Credit: Dover Publications Inc.

Project - You Compose!

You just looked at a picture of a home in 1658. This scene could have happened on any day. Paint a picture of something you see today in your home. Include any people, animals, or objects. Include what is around them like doorways, windows, or sidewalks. 1. Draw with watercolor crayons. Fill in the spaces with color. 2. Dip your brush in water and paint water over the colors.

> **MATERIALS GROUP #2**
> Watercolor crayons, Watercolor paper, Brush

STUDENT GALLERY

Cayla (age 6) draws lines with the watercolor crayons as you can see in the left building. She then fills it in with color and brushes the color with water as seen in the red house with orange windows.

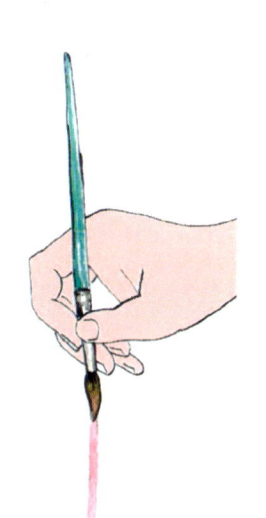

LIKE THIS! Always drag the brush across the paper using just the tip and mid-section to transfer the water to the paper.

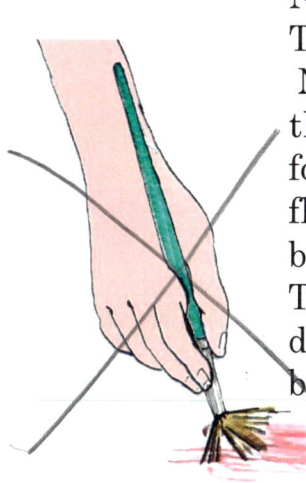

NOT LIKE THIS! Never push the brush forward or flatten the bristles. This damages the brush.

1.

2.

Artists Imagine

Artists imagine. Imagination starts with images, pictures, ideas, or things we see in the world around us. Perhaps you have seen a character in a movie or a book and the character did special things you would like to do. You start with your ideas about this character, perhaps even dressing like him or her. Then you play the part. Soon you can act out new adventures, because you imagine what that character will act like.

An artist begins with an idea of what he or she wants to draw. The artist can add to that idea by looking at pictures or at something in the real world. As the young boy studies the lizard, he pictures in his mind what a larger creature of that nature might look like. What he sees turns to something new through his imagination!

Information Gathering Exercise

Take an information-gathering trip. Walk around your classroom or neighborhood. Gather lots of visual information so that your imagination has many images to work with. Take along a notebook and pencil. Draw the things you see. Write words to help you remember them.

> This lesson teaches us that artists use imagination to create their artwork. They begin with ideas and gather information for pictures.

Look at Imagination
In 20th Century France

In this painting, the artist began with his memories of a birthday. He includes the people, the cake, a bouquet of flowers, and the furniture within the tiny apartment. He did not paint these things in a realistic way, but used his imagination. He imagines objects as they are seen from different angles. The plate and cake are seen from the top, while the cup is seen from the side. The woman's feet do not seem to touch the ground. The man floats in space and his neck is strangely curved to meet her face to face. Marc Chagall does not paint the birthday as someone would see it, but in a way that shows his feelings about the birthday.

Marc Chagall, *The Birthday*, 1915. Photo Credit: Dover Publications Inc.

What birthday gift does the woman hold in her hands?
Look at the window. Is this birthday happening in the daytime or at night?
The woman's foot rests on the bottom of the picture. Do the legs of the table do the same?
How do the man's feet tell us that he is floating in air? How do you think the man feels at the moment? When someone is happy we sometimes say they feel "lighter than air" so they would float off the ground the way Marc Chagall paints himself in this painting.

Project -You Imagine!

You just looked at a picture of a birthday where the artist included imaginative things. Think of a time you enjoyed. Paint it. You can use your imagination to add to the picture in any way you want. You can imagine things in different colors to show your feelings about the special time. Paint with watercolor crayons as shown below.

STUDENT GALLERY

This artwork by Laurel (age 7) shows her experience of her neighborhood. Roller blades, a radio, and a princess crown add to her enjoyment of the moment. Details include hair blowing back in the wind.

1. Begin the artwork in pencil if you want to be able to erase some lines. Use your other hand to hold the paper still as you draw.

2. Once the lines look like you want them to look, color areas with watercolor crayons. Hold the crayons just like you held the pencil.

3. Dip a brush into a can of water. A wide can, like a tuna can, is less likely to spill. Apply the water to the paper. Blend the water and colors to create your painting. Remember to PULL the brush across the paper as you work. Dip the brush in water to keep it wet and to keep the paint pigment flowing.

Artists Look

What kinds of things can you find in a park, meadow, stream, or beach? You may find more than you think when you take time to look carefully. Artists gather information when they look. Then artists draw lines that best describe the information they see. A branch

might be drawn with long thin lines. A seashell might be a round shape with lines spreading out to the edges. Rocks may have smooth surfaces or rough and may be drawn with dots or points to show what the surface looks like. Looking carefully tells us that natural objects are very different from each other and we can draw those differences by using our pencil in different ways.

Seeing Exercise

Without looking, make a list of the objects that you remember seeing from a window in a room. Non-writers can draw pictures of objects. Once you make the word list or picture list, go to the window to observe carefully. How many MORE things can be added to the list using observation?

Note: Help children write the lists, but allow them to find the items. Once they have finished, you can point out other things to open their eyes to even more of what is in front of them.

> This lesson teaches us that artists look at the world to see more details. The art is more interesting when details are drawn.

Look at Nature
In 18th Century France

This painting is by an American artist who studied with the French Impressionists. A popular subject was the painting of fields of poppies found in France. The people in this painting look as though they enjoy being in nature on a warm, sunny day. They sit, look around, and let their minds wander. When you are in a quiet place your mind acts on its own. Many times you get inspired with new thoughts and ideas. In this scene we see a woman and children who are each absorbed with their own thoughts as they look at nature's beauty.

Robert Vonnoh, *In Flanders Field – Where Soldiers Sleep and Poppies Grow*, 1890.
Originally titled, *Coquelicots (Poppies)*, it was renamed in 1919 when the Butler Institute acquired the work. The new name is a reference to the German invasion of Belgium during World War 1, and to the 1915 poem, "In Flanders Fields," by the Canadian surgeon, John McCrae. Photo Credit: Dover Publications Inc.

How many children join the woman in the field?

One child has his back turned away from the viewer. What does he see in the distance? (A farmer sits on a cart pulled by horses.)

How does the artist show that this is a warm, sunny day?

Project -You Look!

You just looked at a picture of children enjoying time in a field of flowers. You can enjoy nature too. Use the lists below to search in nature for objects to draw. This activity can be a nature hunt in your back yard, park, or an inside activity where you observe natural objects that your teacher has brought into the room. Draw what you see on one sheet of paper using pencil.

MATERIALS GROUP #1
Ebony Pencil
Sketch paper
Eraser

Outdoor Nature Hunt List: seedpod, leaf shapes, stick or twig, feather, something soft, something stiff, wild grass, rocks, thorn, wild flower, insect, pinecone, broken egg shell, birds nest, birds, trees, cloud shapes, water, fish, animal.
Note: You may notice that the list has small items that will take careful looking in order to find and larger items we are used to seeing. By looking for the small items, we cause the student to focus attention on the visual skills necessary to locate subjects. Once focused, students notice more in the clouds and trees. It is not necessary to find all these items but to find something interesting within your area.

STUDENT GALLERY

Eira (age 6) saw the shapes of leaves and chose to draw trees and flowering plants from a distance.

Indoor Nature Hunt List: shells, leaves, driftwood, stones, pinecones, seedpods, small mammals or reptiles, fish in a bowl.

Note: Many of these objects can be bought at craft and hobby stores. Once items are obtained, they can be spread in various groups throughout the room so that students can search, look, examine, and then choose their favorite items to draw. They can place the objects anywhere on the page as if taking notes, rather than composing a still-life.

Some students feel a need for color. Don't hesitate to let them add color if they desire it.

Artists Communicate

Did you know that pictures talk? Artists don't make words that we hear with our ears. They make pictures that we see with our eyes and understand. The two children in this picture act very differently toward the dog. Can you tell what has just happened by looking at the children? What is the girl doing with her body? What is the boy doing with his body? The artist tells this story without words. When artists show a body moving or give it action it says a lot!

Communication Exercise

Show gestures. To make a gesture use your body to tell people what you are doing or feeling. Adults can help students by suggesting words that they act out while others observe and make quick sketches of the emotion. Some words to get started are surprised, tired, happy, shocked, scared, excited, sad, hopeful, disappointed, hurried, relaxed, funny, crying, and tickled. If working with one student the adult and student can take turns acting and drawing. Students love this shared experience, and they learn to think about putting expression into their figures of people. At another time you may want to use the exercise with action words such as dig, jump, fall, bounce, pet a pet, hug, squeeze, eat, crawl, look, kneel, sleep, walk, and build. Don't worry about the results or how the drawings look. Learning comes by participating.

> This lesson teaches us that artists talk with pictures. Showing people in action says a lot.

Look at a Picture that Talks
In the Dutch Golden Age of the 17th Century

This picture uses images we all understand. The guests and food tell viewers that this is a party. It is a feast in celebration of a child's Christening. Customs change over the years and vary from country to country. People viewing this painting nearly 400 years ago saw a celebration scene told through a picture. The child is near the center of the picture and wrapped in a red blanket. The white garment underneath helps the child to stand out against the dark room.

Jan Steen *The Christening Feast*, 1664. Photo Credit: Dover Publications Inc. NY

Find the Christened infant. How many people in the room look toward the child?
Women are preparing food. Which women are cooking?
What types of food and cooking utensils lay on the floor?
Can you see the child's bassinet or cradle in the room?

Project -You Talk with Pictures!

MATERIALS GROUP #2
Watercolor crayons
Watercolor paper
Brush, pencil
Can of water
Paper towel

You just looked at a picture that said a lot about the people who were in it. Draw a picture that talks. Add details that tell the viewer who the people in your picture are and what they do. Think about where people work to gather information to use in your painting. Do they wear uniforms or items like boots or gloves? Do they use tools or other equipment?

You may want to visit your local post office, fire station or police station. Observe a waitress, zookeeper, ballet or theatrical performer, street worker, construction worker, farmer, gardener or mechanic. Do not overlook the workers and the opportunities that are near you and easily found!

When creating your picture you may want to draw it with pencil and then use watercolor crayons as shown on page ten.

STUDENT GALLERY

Art by Kari (age 9) was made after returning from a trip to Japan. The costumes, fireworks, and hanging lanterns were a part of her experience while visiting that country.

Art by Kellen (age 7) shows a large gold building that he saw while in Japan. He puts mountains in the background, water in the foreground, and himself in center of the picture. This picture tells people a lot about Kellen's experience.

Artists Use Photographs

Artists use photographs to gather information that would be hard to see in other ways. A photograph can show a still image of two kittens while playing. It can help us see a tiger from far away or help us get a bigger, better view of a tiny ladybug. A camera makes a photograph. The camera captures images that are copied to paper or to a computer screen.

Edgar Degas *Blue Dancers, 1898.*
Photo Credit: Dover Publications, Inc.

Before the invention of photography, artists who could draw a figure when in motion were rare. Artists like Michelangelo in the 1500's were highly praised for this skill. Most artists painted directly from a model that had to sit very still for a very long time. This gave the artist time to paint the form and colors correctly, but it made pictures look stiff and unnatural. In the 1800's, Edgar Degas, an artist, began to use photographs of ballerinas to study their movements. Degas was a talented painter and draftsman who, for a brief time in his career, explored photographs as "studies" or a way to see certain details more closely. See what this painting has in common with typical photographs.

Do the heads of the figures go out of the picture just as we see in quickly taken snapshots?

Do we look down upon the ballerinas as if we sit in a balcony?

Do the ballerinas look as if they are moving while the picture was being painted?

Project -You Use Photos!

Find a photo of a subject you like. Good photos can be found in nature or sports magazines. Look at the details in the photograph and include background objects.

Choose a photograph. Tape the photo beside your drawing paper. Place all the materials within easy reach. Draw what you see in the photo. Color the picture using watercolor crayons, and then add water to blend colors.

STUDENT GALLERY

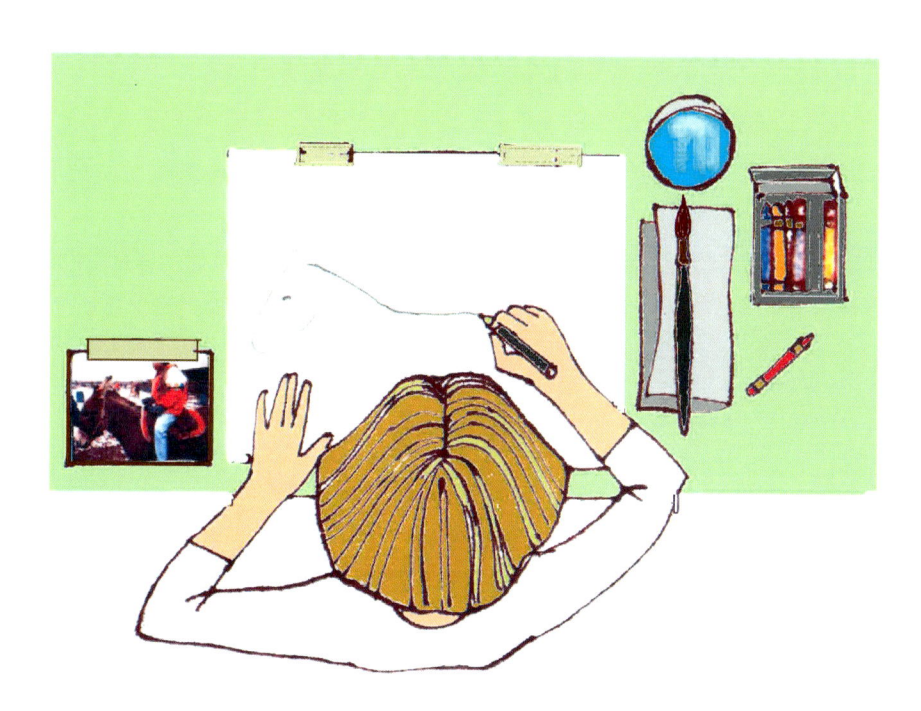

This painting is by Laurel (age 8). She looked at the photo below from a calendar page while she painted the picture.

Always place the brush, water can, and art materials on the side in which you hold your brush. This way they are in easy reach and you won't drip water across the painting.

Artists Plan the Space

Charles Demuth (1883-1935), *Flour Mill*. Photo Credit: Dover Publications Inc.

Artists use lines to plan where the objects will be placed on the space of the paper. Lines show us the edges. Artists use color to fill the space on a canvas or piece of paper. Look at this picture of a factory where flour is made. It is called *Flour Mill* and was painted by Charles Demuth. Can you see lines that show the edges of the buildings? Lines show us the edges of the water towers and the color gray helps them stand out. What do you think the strong diagonal lines show us? Could they be beams of sunlight? These yellow and white streams of light are drawn in the same way as the buildings.

Where do you see parallel lines, lines that go in the same direction with the same distance between them?

Where do you see converging lines, lines that are wide apart but connect at some point?

Where do you see curved lines? Are most of the lines curved or straight?

What object is orange? Does the yellow describe an object or something else? Do you think it describes light?

Parents can help students to become better artists by encouraging them in the following areas:

1. Keep pencils, pens, erasers and paper in a location where the smallest student can reach them easily. If students cannot easily locate the tools needed, they will quickly loose the impetus to draw. That moment of inspiration, which might have turned into a half-hour of working out their ideas on paper, is lost forever.
2. Encourage students to draw subjects that they like. Artistic skills WILL improve the more students draw. Students will draw more when enjoying the process. When students think of their own subject matter and draw from their own preferences, they create, instead of copying something worked out by another individual. They enjoy the process more.

Pencil Drawing

Project -You Use Ebony Pencil!

The Ebony pencil is a super-hero among pencils. It makes a very black mark when you push on the pencil. It covers more area faster because of the wide lead.

STUDENT GALLERY

This drawing is by Shelly (age 5). She composed a picture with two animals and beautiful tall cactus plants.

Hold the pencil between your thumb and index finger and rest the pencil on your middle finger. Move your whole hand and arm as you draw. Your hand will get tired too quickly if you squeeze the pencil too tight or try to draw moving only your fingers.

Draw an object from real life. Then, place it in an imaginary outdoor scene. To draw an object, place it in front of you, just above the paper. Look at the edges. The same edge that you see will be the edge that you draw onto the paper.

Draw the edges in one section at a time. You can erase lines that you don't want with an eraser. Rather than throwing a drawing away when something isn't right, erase and redraw lines on the same sheet of paper. Remember to see the edge, then, draw the edge.

Artists Fill in Spaces

Charles Burchfield (1863-1967) *Childhood's Garden.*
Photo Credit: Dover Publications Inc.

When you draw, you focus on the objects you see and want to put into the picture. You plan your picture by drawing the lines that describe those objects. When you begin to color the picture, you will certainly be excited to add color to those objects. Space around those objects can be colored also. Look at how the artist, Charles Burchfield, fills in the area around the house and trees. This picture of an imaginary garden is filled with plants of many different shapes and colors. In the painting called *Childhood's Garden* every space is filled.

Do you see curved lines? You point to clouds, bushes, and trees.
Do you see straight lines in this picture?

Project -You Fill the Space using Water Color Crayons!

The outdoors is filled with objects. See how to use the watercolor crayons on the next page. Then choose an outdoor scene and fill in the space with colors.

John (age 7) filled in the sky with color in the work at the right. This student artist saw a tree, the sun, bushes, and a large stone. He also filled in the space around those objects with a bright blue sky.

MATERIALS GROUP #2
Watercolor crayons, Watercolor paper, brush, water container, paper towel

STUDENT GALLERY

Watercolor Crayon

The watercolor crayon is paint in a stick. After it is applied to the paper, it can be dissolved with water to create a painting.

To begin, you can draw a picture with pencil if you like to erase and make changes before the color is applied. Once you like where things sit in the picture, apply the colors directly onto the paper.

1. Color the objects. Color the space around the objects. Color can be put on the paper lightly. Color can be put on the paper more heavily by pressing a bit harder as you color.

2. Dip the brush in a can of water. Brush over the colored areas with the wet brush. Brush along the edges carefully. If you brush across two colors, they will blend so do that only where you want to blend colors. The colors appear brighter once water is applied.

1.

2.

In the finished work, some spaces of the paper are left white, but most areas around the cat figurine and water can are filled in.

Heavy marks make darker areas on the finished painting while light marks make lightly colored areas. You can see light and dark areas in the green cloth.

Artists Draw in Color

Ando Hiroshige, Suido Bridge and Surugadai, 1857. Photo Credit: Dover Publications Inc.

Artists draw in color using colored sticks. Applying color to a surface such as a wall or piece of paper has been an activity of mankind that reaches many thousands of years into the past. Today we use pastels as a way of adding color to a picture without using water. In this painting the artist draws a picture in black line and colors in large areas. This painting is called *Suido Bridge and Surugadai.* The title tells us that the artist saw a bridge in the Kanda-Surugadai district of Tokyo, Japan.

Do you see a bridge in the picture?

You probably noticed the fish kite that takes up most of the space in this painting. Can you find other fish kites in the distance?

What other objects do you see in the distance? Look for people, white banners, and a mountain.

Project -You Use Oil Pastels!

Choose underwater subjects, such as fish or sea creatures to put in your art. Draw the objects with a colored or black oil pastel. Fill in the spaces with colors. See the next page to learn how oil pastels can be used by blending colors together.

STUDENT GALLERY

Jessie, (age 8) draws a variety of sea shells.

Oil Pastels

Pastels are a drawing tool with color. Pastels make colored lines. Pastels can be used to fill in areas of solid color. Oil pastels can be used like crayons, however they are softer and that gives them a special ability to blend. When applied thickly to the paper, one color can be pressed onto another and the two colors mix.

1. Begin by drawing your picture in pencil. You can erase the pencil and make changes. Once you like your drawing, begin to color in the shapes with oil pastel colors. If a stick breaks, simply use the smaller pieces. Peel back the paper on the stick when it wears down.

2. Blend colors that are similar to each other such as the light and dark orange shown in the fish scale.

3. Fill in all the spaces as shown in the final drawing.

1.

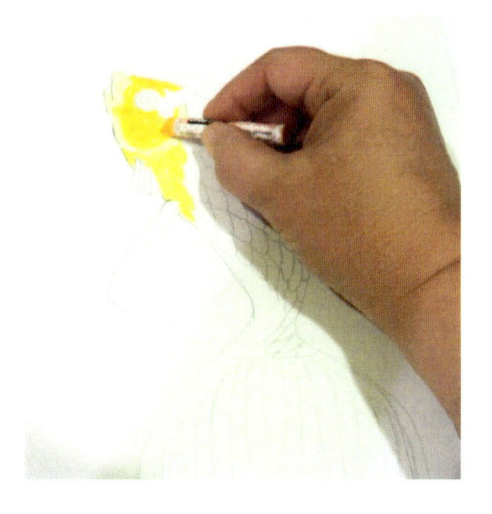

2.

3.

Artists Outline Shapes

Edgar Degas Rider in a Red Coat, 1873. Photo Credit: Dover Publications Inc. NY

When you draw with a material that has color, such as soft pastels, you must choose a color for the lines. These lines add beauty to your finished art. Look at this picture of a jockey. A jockey is a man that rides a racehorse. The picture is called *Rider in Red Coat.* It was painted by Edgar Degas in 1873. In it we can see the outlines of the horse that the man sits on. The outline is a line that shows the edge of the object so that it can be recognized. The artist did not finish this work so we can see the way he started it. He has filled in the lines describing the coat with red color. If he had continued on this painting, a color would have been chosen for the horse too.

What stands out most in this painting of a man on a horse?

Does the red coat stand out because of its color or because it is in the center of the page?

Do you think both of these characteristics of the coat help it to be the center of attention?

Project: You Use Soft Pastels!

Use colored pastels to draw a picture in color. Choose an animal from a photograph. Look at the photograph to see the shape of the animal. Look at the photograph to get information that you can put into your picture. See the next page for tips on how to use soft pastels.

STUDENT GALLERY

Annora age (6) draws the kangaroo, first with white pastels, and then fills in the areas with color.

25

Soft Pastels

Soft pastels are a chalk-like material and may also be called chalk pastels. These materials look great when applied to colored or black paper. This background makes the colors stand out. 1. For this drawing made from soft pastel, the artist broke down the parts into small shapes that fit onto each other. The round nose shape is on top of the round head shape. The round head shape fits onto the rounded body shape. Then the shapes of the ears were added. 2. The pastels are used to fill in the shapes. Colors are layered over other colors to mix. Dark brown, pink, and white were used here. 3. In the last stage of the soft pastel drawing, the background is added. Some of the black paper shows through the green and blue.

Parent's Note: The soft pastel will fall off the paper unless it is fixed to it. To fix the pigments hold the paper about 12 inches from a can of hairspray and give the entire work a light coating of hairspray. It will curl immediately, but straighten out on its own once it dries.

1.

2.

3.

Artists Make Landscapes

Paul Cézanne *Monte Sainte-Victoire above the Tholonet Road*,
1896-98. Photo Credit: Dover Publications Inc.

A landscape is a nature scene showing the outdoors. In art, a landscape can be drawn with a pencil or painted to show the colors of the land, water, or sky. Paul Cézanne painted this mountain repeatedly during his lifetime. It is titled *Monte Sainte-Victoire above the Tholonet Road*, 1896-98. Look at all the colors he used in the mountain, the trees, and the earth. He used the paint in a way that looks like the oil pastels that you will use in your next work of art.

What objects do you see in this landscape?
Which objects take up the most space in the painting? (mountain range)
Which objects take up little space in the painting? (house, some trees)
What spaces are filled, but are not actual objects? (sky, ground)

MATERIALS GROUP #1
Oil Pastels
Sketch paper

Project: You Make a Landscape!

You make a landscape in color. Go outdoors on a comfortable day. Using oil pastels draw and color a picture of what you see. Read about shape and size on the next page. Use these ideas in your picture. Ben created a very large tree in his picture of a fruit tree.

STUDENT GALLERY

This grand fruit tree with houses in the background was seen and created by Ben (age 5).

27

Shapes and Sizes

Consider SHAPE. When you look at objects and draw them there is a lot of information to take in. Artists often try to simplify this information in their minds. The trees at the right are already simplified from the original tree, but they can be simplified even more. Can you find which trees most closely resemble the simple shapes below?

Consider SIZE. It is easiest to show the size of a tree when it is placed by other objects that are recognizable and similar in size. The two figures below the pine tree on the left show that this is a very large tree. The single figure beside the tree on the right shows that this tree is much smaller. You can use objects in your picture to show how big a tree is.

Artists Make Portraits

Hans Holbein the Younger, *Henry VIII*, 1539-40. Photo Credit:
Dover Publications Inc.

Pictures of people are called portraits. A portrait may show much more about a person than what he looks like. The artist may surround the person with objects or may use the clothing or hairstyle to tell us more about the person. The artist may place the person in a special setting. In this portrait of *Henry VIII*, painted by Hans Holbein the Younger, there is no special setting because the King himself is grander than anything else is in the world. His body fills the space from top to bottom and side to side. His clothing speaks of his greatness. Clothing was a luxury item and only a king could afford the firs, jewels, medallions, silks, and the quantity of rich fabric shown here.

Many portraits are drawn from the side during this time period. What direction does the king face for this portrait?

Find jewels in this picture. Find white tufts of expensive fur on the jackets. How is his clothing different from what men wear today?

Project: You Draw a Face!

You paint a portrait using watercolor crayons, watercolor paper, and a brush. Look at a person, or prop up a mirror and set it in front of you as you draw.

Your portrait will not look like the drawing below, however, you can learn a few things about where to start.

If we mark the top of the head and the bottom of the chin, notice that the eyes sit in the middle of those two lines. To draw a head, make an oval.

Mark the center of the oval with a light line. Place the eyes there. Draw the nose and mouth under that. Add hair. Sometimes the forehead will show.

Also look at the way the hair sits almost like a helmet, encircling the head.

STUDENT GALLERY

Kyle (age 6) paints a picture of a friend and fills in the background with colorful marks.

Artists Make Still-Lifes

Vincent van Gogh, Still Life with Coffeepot, 1888.
Photo Credit: Dover Publications Inc.

How many lemons are in the picture?

Are they all facing the same direction?

Can you find a checkered pot?

How many pots have handles?

How many small cups are in the picture?

Can we say that the objects are very different from each other, having variety?

MATERIALS GROUP #2
watercolor crayons
watercolor paper
brush, water container

Project: You Paint a Still Life!

Set three objects together on a table. See the next page to learn how to use three objects in a picture. Look at the objects and color a picture of them with watercolor crayons.

Artists choose special objects and arrange them on a tabletop to be painted. Objects are chosen that give artists the colors or subject matter they want to work with. We call this kind of painting a "still-life" because the objects stay still. They don't move around like an animal or a person does. The subject became popular during the Reformation as people searched for subjects that could express religious ideas without using religious figures. Objects stood for ideas like humbleness, generosity, prosperity, etc. Today artists continue to paint objects, but rarely do the objects have special meanings or express ideas beyond what they are. This still-life titled, *Still Life with Coffeepot,* is by Vincent Van Gogh. The painting shows simple objects spread out on a table top with a bright yellow wall in the background.

STUDENT GALLERY

Jack (age 5) paints a fish bowl with shells.

Arrangement of Three Objects

A good still-life picture has in it things that are the same and things that are different. Follow these ideas for good design.

Choose three objects that are the same or similar. Make them different by angling them in different directions. See that the apples do not all set upright in this picture. You can place one apple in front of another so that the one furthest from you is partly covered up. This is called overlap. Overlap is another way to make a picture interesting.

The cups are placed in different directions in this group. With open objects like these cups, one object can be placed inside the other. The cups overlap. Can you point to the parts of the cups that are hidden or covered up by another cup?

Your picture will look great when you follow these ideas of changing angles and overlap.

Artists Draw Figures

George Caleb Bingham, The Jolly Flatboatmen, 1864.
Photo Credit: Dover Publications Inc.

When people move, the arms and legs extend further from their bodies. Which man shows the most movement in this painting? Where do the arms bend? Where do the legs bend? When drawing, why is it important to bend your figures at the elbows and knees?

The things we do and the things that happen to us are good subjects to show in art. Experiences became a subject for painting during the early 1800's in America. George Caleb Bingham painted this work titled, *The Jolly Flatboatmen,* in 1864. Bingham spent much time on the Mississippi River along with men like those shown in his picture. Eight men enjoy a rousing dance as the violinist plays his tune. The flatboat floats down this calm section of the great river. The Mississippi River is like a great highway, especially in the 1800's. It is used to transport goods from the north, as far as Minnesota, to the Gulf of Mexico.

STUDENT GALLERY

Antoine (age 8) experienced a ride in a boat. He remembers many details. The sun's hot rays shine down on the passengers. The water sprays up the side of the boat.

MATERIALS GROUP #2
Watercolor crayons
Watercolor paper
Brush, Pencil

Project: You Draw Figures!

Make a painting with watercolor crayons that shows an experience you have had. Show what you felt, saw, and heard. Put figures in the painting. To learn more about figures see the next page.

Contour Edges

A contour is the edge you see that separates the object from what is around it. Artists draw this edge to show an image of the object on paper. You have probably already looked at contours as you draw. When you become more aware of the edge, you can draw with more confidence. Some students still use stick figures when drawing a human. By looking at the contour, you can see that the arms and legs are more than sticks that are drawn with a single line. More lines are needed.

To understand more about how human figures are constructed, you can draw a model or figure commonly found in the toy box or sitting on your shelves.

Children see and draw people in a variety of interesting ways when we allow them to make their own decisions. Many children never draw a stick figure or draw only parts of the body in those ways. A young child may start with a stick figure, as in the student work above, and "dress" the figure adding fullness in the clothing. You may want to help a child see that the arms and legs have two outside edges by pointing to your own body and running your hand across the top and bottom of an extended arm, however they will usually make these discoveries on their own when taught to observe real people.

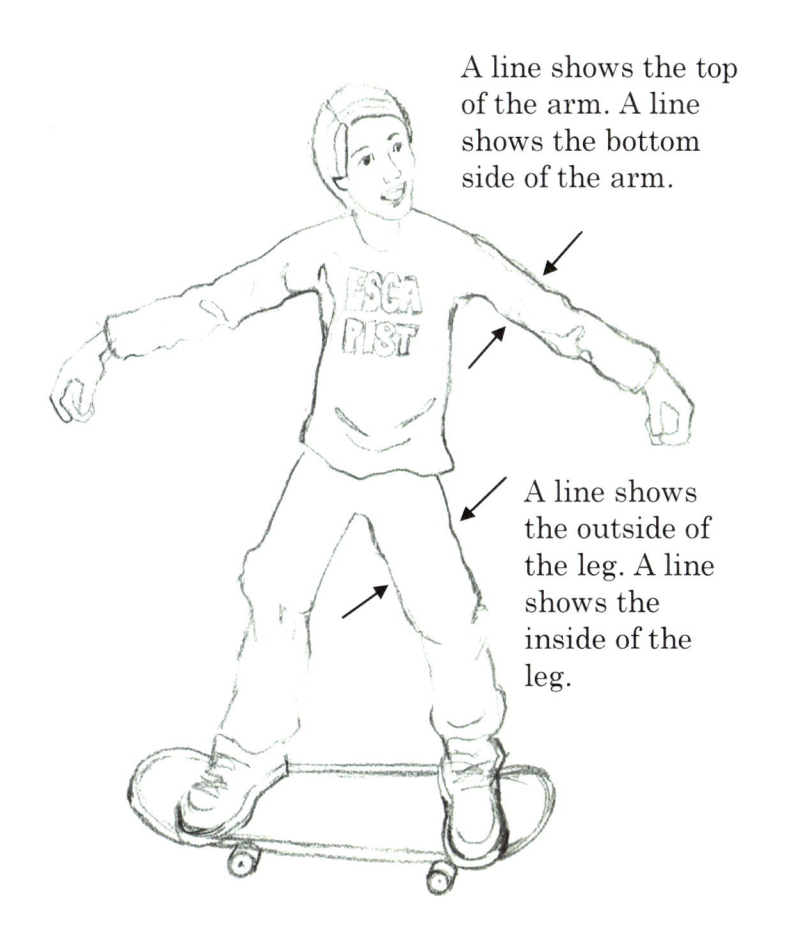

A line shows the top of the arm. A line shows the bottom side of the arm.

A line shows the outside of the leg. A line shows the inside of the leg.

Artists Show Works

Samuel F. B. Morse, *Gallery of the Louvre*. Photo Credit: Dover Publications Inc., NY.

Project: You Draw!

Make a picture for display using soft pastels on colored construction paper. Read the next page to see how to have an opening by displaying art and inviting people to see it.

> **MATERIALS GROUP #2**
> Chalk pastels,
> Colored construction Paper

STUDENT GALLERY

Ben (age 6) drew a scene of himself on a volcano that he visited with his family. The dark blue matte makes his picture stand out.

Athletes or musicians often practice alone but perform in front of people. The artist often practices and completes artwork alone. In order for people to see the art, the artist must invite people to a show of the work. The first day of a show is called an opening because the artist opens the door to the studio or gallery, inviting people to look. People come to look at the artwork and talk to the artist. The artist answers any questions people might have. They might ask how the work was made or what it was made from. They might ask what kinds of ideas inspired the artist to make the work. Artists show works in many places like art galleries, art museums, coffee shops, and restaurants. If you were an artist in the 19th century, you would want to have your work displayed at the Salon in Paris. The Salon exhibited paintings from floor-to-ceiling and on every available foot of space, as you can see in the painting by Samuel F.B. Morse, *Gallery of the Louvre*.

What kinds of activities are people doing in this gallery room?

Are they interacting with the paintings?

Your Opening Show

Plan a show of your works following these steps:

1. Choose your best artworks.
2. Frame these works as shown below.
3. Plan a time to show the work. Invite people to come to see your work.
4. Hang your works on a wall, bulletin board, etc. Hang the pictures at eye level.
5. Plan snacks and drinks if desired.
6. When people arrive at your Opening, talk about your work. Talk about what inspired you to make it, how you used the materials, etc.

FRAMING YOUR WORK: Make a simple frame from construction paper that is slightly larger than the paper your artwork is on. You can glue two pieces of paper together if necessary, to make a larger sheet. The paper frame should be darker or of a different color than the original artwork. This will make the artwork stand out. Carefully turn the original artwork over. With the glue stick, dab the four corners or run a line of glue around the four sides. Turn it over and carefully place it in the center of the frame. Press gently over the glued areas. Do not smear the picture by rubbing it. Use a third piece of paper over the drawing, and then press down on the glued areas.

construction paper matte artwork extra sheet for pressing

Note: Showing works can be as simple as displaying on a wall or bulletin board what students have done so far. Take a few moments to acknowledge what they've done. Doing this will give students a sense of accomplishment. You may want to encourage a show for family members when students have finished this book. A small show at this point will greatly heighten their anticipation for a bigger, better show and create a sense of purpose for their art.

Artists See Shapes

Lesson 15

Everything has shape. You can identify many things by their shapes. Botanists identify trees by the shapes of their flat leaves. Round things can be identified by their shapes too. Try to identify the three fruits below by their shapes.

Shape shows us how tall and how wide an object is, but does not show roundness. You could not see the roundness or color of the fruit, yet you were able to identify the objects easily. Shape tells us a lot about what we are looking at.

Shape Exercise

When leaves are available, gather a variety of leaf shapes. Place each leaf on colored construction paper. Trace around the edges of the leaves. Cut out the shapes and arrange the paper shapes together on a separate sheet of construction paper, which is different in color from the leaf shapes.

Note: Encourage children to cut out what they really see, not simplified versions of the object. If the leaf has a jagged edge, they should attempt to cut a jagged edge, as well as the overall shape. Point these details out in the chosen object. This may be a new skill for children so do not be critical of their efforts. We want to create awareness of shapes, not perfection in the results.

> This lesson teaches us that artists show shape by using areas that are different from the area behind it, making it stand out.

Look at Shapes
In 20th Century Mexico

Shapes are flat. Some shapes like circles, squares and triangles are easy to recognize. Shapes that describe natural forms such as flowers, animals, or people must be observed carefully. This scene of a peddler selling flowers for Flower Day is painted using simple natural shapes. The shape of each flower is repeated. Look at the flower shapes. Colors can show us the edges of a shape. Leaf shapes are shown in green. Each woman's blouse is shown in white. Hair is shown in black.

Can you find the shapes shown below within the picture?

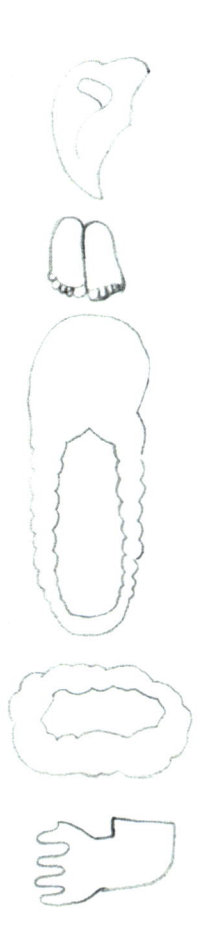

Diego Rivera, *Flower Day*, 1925
Photo Credit: Dover Publications Inc.

What color are the flowers the peddler holds in his hands?

Can you find a wreath of flowers in that same color?

Project -You See Shapes!

Make a paper cutout collage. Look at an outdoor scene. Draw shapes of the objects you see then cut them out and glue them to the background colors. You can cut the shapes out directly without drawing first. See shapes that go beyond a circle, square, rectangle or triangle. Look at the outside edge of objects for unusual shapes.

STUDENT GALLERY

Shannon (age 7) made this work after a heavy snow had fallen. She noticed that the snow sat on top of tree branches.

1. Cut out a shape for the ground.

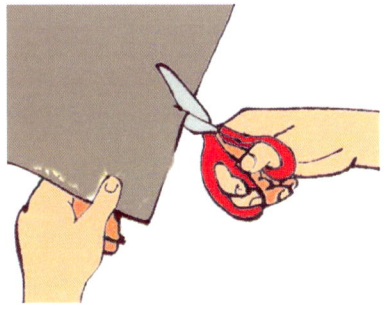

2. Glue the ground shape onto the background sheet.

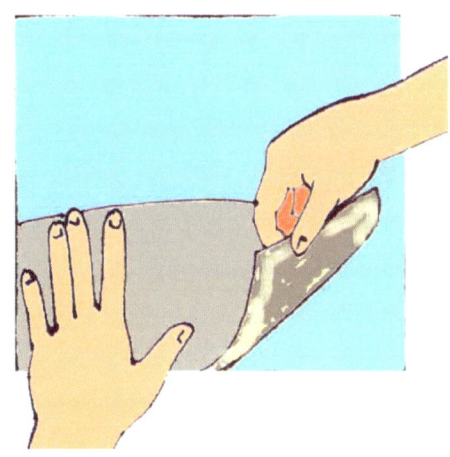

3. Cut out big shapes. Glue them onto the background.

4. Cut small shapes. Glue smaller shapes on top of the big shapes. Draw any details you want to add. A bird and some people were drawn in this picture.

Artists See Form

It is easiest to understand form when we compare it to shape. A circle cut from a piece of paper has shape and is a flat object. A baseball has the same shape but it is not flat. It is rounded and has form. Paper dolls look real from the front, but turned to the side they no longer resemble a person at all. They are only shapes. Most other dolls have form. A picture is made on paper, a flat shape. The images look real, but they are not rounded as they look, only flat. Sculpture is a name for art that is rounded – having form. Sculptures can

be found on buildings or standing alone. Sculptures can be small enough to fit in your hand or as large as the Statue of Liberty. These forms can be made of wood, metal, stone, marble, clay or other material. The actual statue of two bear cubs, shown above, is a sculpture. The sculpture has form so the girl can touch all sides, walk around, or sit on the bear.

Shape and Form Exercise

Using a piece of paper, bring the two ends together to make a tube. Tape the ends and set the tube upright on the table. You just made a shape into a form. With paper, scissors and tape make other forms. You may cut, fold, tear and bend to make interesting forms.

> This lesson teaches us that form is different from shape because it shows roundness. Artists who use form in their art create sculptures.

Look at Form
In 20th Century France

Forms have height, width and depth just like you. Your height is from your head to your toes. Your width is from shoulder to shoulder. Your depth is from your chest to your back. This sculpture of a boy and bear is a form that can be touched. We could touch the bumpy edge of the top of the fence. We could run our hands over the jacket, moving in and out of the folds. We could run our fingers over the bear's back and feel the curves and the ears that stick up. We can only do these activities with something that has form.

How is this form different from a painting?

The boy plays a musical instrument called bagpipes. Have you seen something like this before?

Is the young bear friendly, afraid, or fierce?

Are they in a forest or town? What object tells you this?

Artist Unknown. *Boy with bagpipes and young bear.* Biscuit porcelain from France. 20th CE. Location: Private Collection, Vienna, Austria Photo Credit: Erich Lessing / Art Resource, NY

Project -You Use Form!

Create an animal with form. Make any four-legged animal using the following steps.

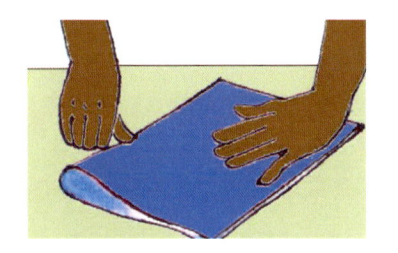

1. Fold paper by bending one edge to meet the opposite edge. Holding the two edges with one hand, rub your thumb along the other edge to make a fold.

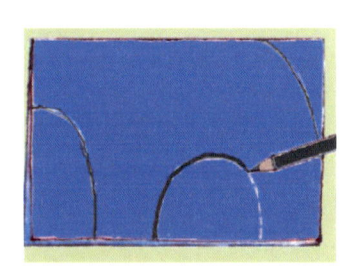

2. With the fold at the top, draw lines similar to the ones shown to create leg, neck, and the back of the animal.

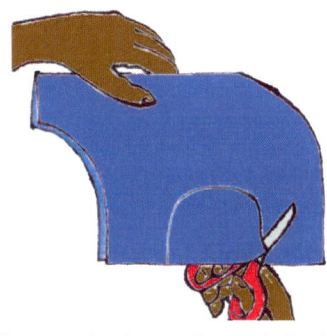

3. Cut on the lines through both sides of the paper. Do not cut the fold! Unfold the paper. Make the next marks on the inside.

4. Mark lines in the center of all legs. Mark an oval shape coming to points on the fold line. Score the paper so that it can be folded on the lines. Do this by pressing firmly over the lines with a ballpoint pen. Do not tear through the paper.

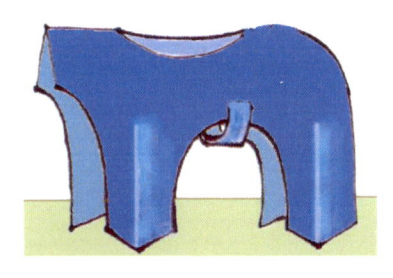

5. Fold the paper on the scored lines keeping the lines to the inside. Cut a strip of paper and glue it to the undersides to make the form stand up.

6. Fold another piece of paper for the head. Draw the shape using the fold for the top of the head. Cut out.

7. Use a glue stick to glue the head to the body. Cut and fold other parts of the animal and glue them onto it. Ears, horns, tails, and elephant trunks can all be cut and glued onto the animal head and body.

Artists See Line

Lines are all around us. Telephone and power lines hang above the ground. Spiders weave thin lines of webs in hidden places. You grab two lines when you swing. Highways have white and yellow lines. With a pencil, one can draw the lines seen in string or a garden hose. But drawing lines that can be seen and touched is not the only way artists use line.

Line can show the outside edge of objects: their shapes. Look at the two lines on the left. Can you see which one follows the face of a man and which one follows the face of a child? Faces do not have lines, but the artist uses line to show the outside edge of the faces.

We can look for lines in prints like the one below. This woodcut shows outlines drawn around the tree branches and the warrior Hero Minamoto no Yoshitsune. Some objects are not outlined. Look at the pine needles. Instead of a line drawn around the outside edge, lines are used to create each pine needle. Lines show pattern on the elaborate costume. Lines show folds in the fabric that the horse is draped in.

Can you find lines in the tree?

What kind of animal appears on the Warrior Hero's helmet?

Look for pattern. Do you see stripes? Do you see flower patterns?

What type of ground do you think the horse is standing on? How do the lines help describe this rough and bumpy path?

Kiyohiro, *The Warrior Hero Minamoto no Yoshitsune*, late 1750's. Photo Credit: Dover Publications Inc.

Project -You Use Line!

Draw a model of a horse, boat, car, figurine, or other object. With your pencil on the paper and your eyes on the object you are drawing, follow the curves of the lines you see. Follow the outside edge of the object. You are drawing its contour. Artists practice this skill all their lives. By practicing contour drawing, you train your hand to follow what your eyes see.

You can use the pencil in another way. Draw lines back and forth to fill in areas with the side of the pencil lead. Hold the pencil under your hand as shown here.

STUDENT GALLERY

This drawing is by Kellen (age 7). The turtle was drawn from a live animal. He fills in the space using the side of the pencil as shown below.

MATERIALS GROUP #1
Ebony Pencil
Sketch paper

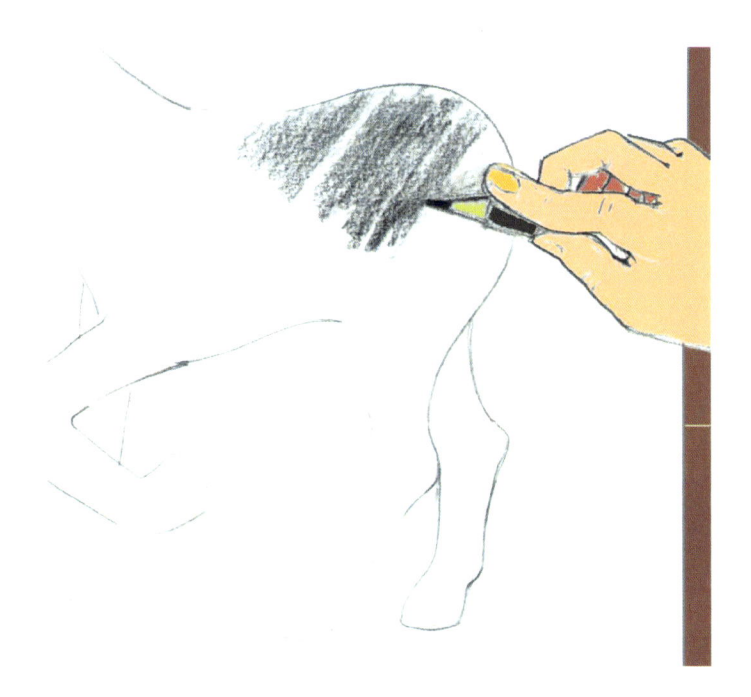

Artists See Color

When something is not black, white, or gray, we say it has color. Color tells us many things. A green light tells people to go. A yellow sign means, "Be careful". A bright blue sky shows good weather.

We identify things by color. A red fruit is probably an apple, strawberry or raspberry. Oranges are described by their color, orange. When a person has a red face, we might associate an emotion with the color. Perhaps they are angry or embarrassed.

Some people have a favorite color. The color blue may make someone feel peaceful. The colors orange and yellow may make someone feel energetic or think about fall, their favorite time of year.

So colors can tell us things, help us identify things or make us feel certain ways. You can use color in your art to help identify the subject or make someone feel a certain way.

Blue

Green

Yellow

Orange

Red

Brown

Color Exercise

Make a picture in color, using colors in at least one of the three ways mentioned. You might make a picture of a car at a stoplight. Use color to show the color of the car and the stoplight to tell if the car is moving or stopping. You might make a picture of fruit using color to identify the kind of fruit. You may make a picture of a winter day using blues and violets to make us feel cold or calm.

This lesson tells us three ways color is used:
1. To tell us something.
2. To help us identify things.
3. To make us feel a certain way.

45

Look at Color
In 19th Century France

Color is all around us. It affects what we do. If you look out the window and see a bright blue sky, you may decide to play in the yard. If the sky is gray, you may decide to stay in. The color of the sky communicated to you. This artist painted fog. The early morning sun breaks through the fog and scatters gold, red and purple light through the sky and onto the water.

Claude Monet, *Houses of Parliament, London, Sun Breaking through the Fog*, 1904
Photo Credit: Dover Publications Inc.

Have you ever seen a foggy morning or evening? How does fog affect what we see?

Here the buildings have blurry edges. What color do they appear?

Does the artist use any lines in this painting or do the colors blur together?

Project -You use Color!

MATERIALS GROUP #2
Watercolor crayons
Watercolor paper
Brush
Pencil
Scissors

You can make new colors by mixing red, blue, and yellow in certain ways. With just three colors, you can have six colors. Cut one sheet of watercolor paper into three strips. Color one strip yellow then color red lightly over it. Brush on water to see what color appears. Do you see orange? Color one strip yellow then color blue lightly over it. Brush on water to see what color appears. Do you see green? Color one strip red then color blue over it. Brush on water to see what color appears. Do you see purple?

STUDENT GALLERY

Look at the rich colors Kara (age 6) obtained by layering colors to get browns and greens. She puts lots of color onto the page. If your colors are pale, try pushing harder to get more pigment on the paper before blending with a brush and water.

1. Place one color on top of another to mix.

2. Blend with water and a brush to make a new color.

Make a painting using your newly discovered color mixtures.

Note: Color sets come with different blues, reds, and yellows, which all mix differently. Do not worry about pure bright green, purple, or orange. For this lesson we want children to see how the colors they choose mix. If their set has several blues, reds, or yellows, have children try each of them and talk about the mixtures that they like best. Children love these discoveries.

Artists See Edges

Hokusai, *Lilies*. Photo Credit: Dover Publications Inc.

Artists make contour drawings. A contour drawing is one where the artist draws the outside edges of the object. This Japanese colored woodblock print titled, *Lilies*, by Hokusai shows the edges of the flowers in black. This black edge shows the contour of each flower petal so that we can clearly see the shape. Some people learn to draw a flower by creating a center then making each petal the same shape as it attaches to the center. Does Hokusai do that? No, he does not. He looks at the actual flower from one position and draws the shape of each petal as he sees it from that position. As you move around the edges look different. For this reason, be still as you draw from observing a real object. This way the edges will remain the same.

How many leaves are in this painting? Do any of them look exactly alike?

How many petals are on the flower that is in the low center of the picture?

Do any of the petals on this flower look exactly alike?

STUDENT GALLERY

Student work by Laurel (age 5) shows the contour of three cats.

Project: You Make A Contour Drawing!

Contour drawings are fun, crazy, and sometimes unrecognizable. Do not make corrections on contour drawings. A contour drawing is practice in **seeing** and gaining **eye/hand coordination**. When you draw this way, you will begin to see that an object has thickness that is defined by its edges.

Notice how the student's eye remains on the contour of the plastic giraffe even as she draws the contour.

Set a large stuffed toy or plastic animal in front of you. To practice drawing the edge, hold your pencil in the air about 12 inches from the toy and (in the air) draw around the outside edge of the toy. Now you know where to look. This time, keeping your eyes on the toy, follow its contour as you draw lines on paper. Your hand should follow where your eye is going as your eye stays on the object, following its edges. You may want to practice using toys with different kinds of contours. Plastic animal figures work well because they are more like real animal forms.

While contour drawing is a traditional way of drawing, the use of drawing in the air to introduce the idea to young people is a new twist and has worked wonderfully with the children I teach. Credit for this idea belongs to Dr. Marvin Bartel, ED.D. teacher at Goshen College Art Department. See: Themes of Development through Art, www.goshen.edu, 06/23/06.

Artists See Space

John Singer Sargent 1856-1925), *Carnation, Lily, Lily, Rose.*
Photo Credit: Dover Publications Inc.

You are probably familiar with outer space, an area beyond the earth that goes on and on without end or edges. On earth, we usually talk about spaces that do end or have edges. Your house sits on a space. Its edges are the outside walls. The paper you draw on is a space with edges. Space is the area between or around the things on your paper.

Artists think about how they will use the space of the paper before drawing on it. Sometimes an artist has one thing to draw and shows only it, leaving the surrounding space empty. The empty space says, "Hey, look over here!" and we immediately notice the object that is surrounded by space. Or the artist may have a lot to show and choose to fill up the space with objects or color. The full space keeps our eyes moving throughout the picture. In this artwork, *Carnation, Lily, Lily, Rose*, by John Singer Sargent we see two girls standing in a garden with sticks and lanterns. The tall flowering plants surround them. Blooms fill the space of the page.

How many lanterns are in this painting? Which girl is in the center of the space?

50

Project: You Fill up the Space!

Parent Preparation Note! Find a source of visual information on a topic such as sea life, animals of the forest, etc. Short, children's science videos or photographs you have gathered from children's nature magazines work well. Show the images to students and ask them to make a picture that shows many of the subjects they saw in the visual information presented. Our purpose for showing a short video is to bring interesting subject matter into the home or classroom as the inspiration for a picture and to challenge the student to remember details and put them into a drawing. Students learn to pay close attention to visual information when they know that they will be drawing that information.

STUDENT GALLERY

BIG WAVE by Kellen (age 6) and UNDER THE SEA by Ariel (age 6).

We are going to look at pictures about (your chosen topic). Watch carefully. You will make a picture that shows some of the things you see.

Think about the (topic) you just saw in the (film) (book) (pictures). Fill the paper with things you remember.

Artists See Texture

Gustav Klimt (1862-1918) *The Sunflower*. Photo Credit: Dover Publications Inc.

Artists learn to look at the world in certain ways. You can see what artists see when you know what to look for. Texture is everywhere in our world. Because objects have different surfaces, we can be aware of those surfaces when we draw them. In the painting, *The Sunflower*, by Gustav Klimt, the paint is applied thickly to show the leafy hedge in the background and other textured surfaces. Dabs of paint are applied to the paper on top of other colors. The texture of the hedge appears rough or bumpy.

What type of object is the main subject of this painting? Are there any objects in the background?

Because of the texture, does the background seem empty or full? Does the background seem plain or active? We can describe textures in many different ways. We can also paint textures in many different ways.

Project: You See Textures in Nature!

Look for textures outdoors. You may see them on the ground or in the trees and bushes. Draw what you see as you sit outdoors. Use the ideas below to get texture into your drawing.

STUDENT GALLERY

This picture by Allen (age 7) uses the oil pastels heavily. Allen drew it while observing the trees outdoors. He noticed that the sky is usually darker up high and lighter as it goes near the horizon.

Select a scene that has objects with texture or repeated patterns. Outline the objects in color. Fill in spaces with color.

Layer other colors on top. This creates the look of texture. The most textured areas in this picture are the tree leaves, sky, and flowering bush.

Where We Find Art This section is designed to expand children's ideas about what art is and where it is found. It introduces children to ancient art and provides opportunities to explore new media. It follows art history from cave paintings to the Middle Ages, as children look at the many places we find art.

Art in Caves

Have you ever dreamed of making a great discovery? In France, four boys discovered some of the oldest art known to the world. They were enjoying a romp through the countryside with their dog, Robot. Suddenly Robot disappeared. They called for him, but could not see him anywhere. Their search led to a deep hole that had been hidden by bushes. The oldest boy descended into the darkness with only some matches he had in his pocket to light the way. He found Robot! Robot had fallen through a crack in the ground. The next day the boy and his friends, along with their school teacher, returned with lights and went down into the 50-foot hole. There they saw oxen, horses, and deer drawn in motion on the walls and ceilings of the cave. Cave art is found throughout the world. We see human figures, animals, tools, maps, and symbols such as circles or hands in caves. Animals found in cave art include extinct ones like cave lions, saber-toothed tigers, mammoths, and horned buffalo. Pictures also include animals we are more familiar with like horses, bears, bison, reindeer, wild boars, fish, and birds. The four boys in our story were not the only children to discover drawings in caves. Many accounts of discovering cave art tell of children who saw the art first (Casteret). Pictures of the cave's interior can be seen in this article: "Art Treasures from the Ice Age: Lascaux Cave" by Rigaud, Jean – Philippe.

This lesson tells us that a discovery by four boys revealed some of the oldest art we know of. Paintings in caves were protected from elements that usually destroyed them like the weather, erosion, or people. We can still see them today!

Look at Cave Art
In Ancient France

Cave art is drawn directly onto the cave walls. Caves protect the art from wind, rain, and natural erosion. That is why we can still see it. Some of the animals are simply outlined in black and others are filled in with bright earth colors, found in nearby rocks and minerals. The first men to document the art had a hard task getting to it. They had to climb on their hands and knees to enter some caverns. The cave floors were uneven and slippery and the spaces were very tight. The animals shown below are painted on the ceiling of a cavern. There are many caverns in the cave at Lascaux. The photograph below shows one section of a long area that is full of bulls, horses, and deer.

Can you find a red horse with a black neck and head? The line extending from the head is really the back of a bull. Can you see the outline of a bull with long horns?

Do the animals seem to be standing or running?

Black horses prance along the bottom of the group. What do you notice about the size of the animals? Find the small red deer with large antlers painted below the nose of the bull.

Great Hall of the Bulls, reconstruction of Paleolithic rock paintings, Lascaux caves, France Photo Credit: Gianni Dagli Orti / The Art Archive at Art Resource, NY Musee des Antiquites St Germain en Laye

Project -You Make Cave Art!

MATERIALS GROUP #1
Soft pastels, earth colors only
Brown wrapping paper
Black construction paper

Sometimes cave art is carved into a rock or wall, but in the caves of France, the art is drawn onto the wall. The artists did not change the surface of the rock, but looked at the bumpy surface to see what sort of animal it suggested. The shapes of some of the animals follow the natural shape of the rock so the body might follow a bump or a crack. You can make a cave picture, using the wrinkles on a piece of paper as your cave wall.

1. Wrinkle a piece of brown paper by crunching it into a loose ball. Carefully flatten it out. Now you have a rough surface similar to what the cave painters drew on.

2. Look for shapes or lines that suggest an animal or part of an animal. The painters of the caves drew animals they saw. Draw an animal you know about using rust, black, brown, yellow, and white soft pastels.

3. When finished, have an adult spray the drawing lightly with hair spray to keep the drawing from smearing.

4. Glue the drawing onto black construction paper. A pattern can be drawn onto the black border with pastel and sprayed again with hair spray.

STUDENT GALLERY

Mommy and baby giraffe are drawn by Amanda (age 6). Giraffes are seen in cave art from Africa.

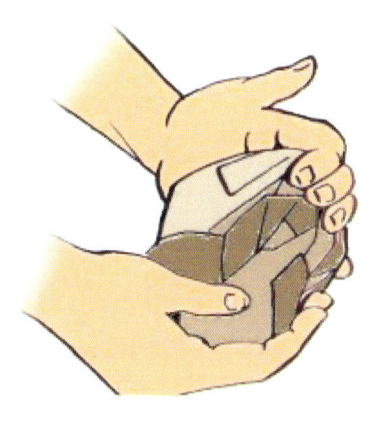

Art Underground
Near- Eastern Pottery

The oldest forms of three dimensional art that have been discovered are half sized human statues, real skulls that have been filled with plaster to form a face, and fragments of pottery. These items were found at different depths in the ground. People dig in excavation sites at Jericho in Jordon to discover how people lived long ago. Jericho is the oldest inhabited town in the world. Digging deep into the ground, archaeologists found the pottery fragments shown below. People formed pots from clay and then scratched into the surfaces to decorate them.

The three foot high statue shown here is one of fifteen found in a large pit. They were discovered when a bulldozer dug a hole for a road at Ain-Ghazal, Jordan in the 1980's. It is made from a mixture of lime-plaster, crushed chalk, and sand. The people who made this long ago also plastered their mud homes with lime-plaster. This clay-like substance was formed over a bundle made of reeds. Reeds are thick grasses. The reed bundle gave the clay-like substance something to be formed around, making the object sturdy. Can you find knees on this statue? Can you find toes? The eyes look like eyes in paintings by the Samarians, but the face is more detailed. Can you find arms? Why do you think there are no arms? They may have been made of something that disintegrated over time or perhaps they were not considered an important part of the body.

One of the oldest known human statues modeled from lime-plaster, crushed chalk and sand over an armature of reed-bundles. Found in 1983-85 at Ain-Ghazal, Jordan. Neolithic
Photo Credit: Erich Lessing / Art Resource, NY
Archaeological Museum, Amman, Jordan

Project -You Make a Figure!

The clay-like figure you just looked at was one of the first types of statues people made. You can make a human figure for perhaps the first time. It can be made from clay or dough. Instead of using a bundle of reeds to support the body, we use a cardboard tube. You can bind up a small bundle of reeds with string, if you have grasses available to you.

To make dough, boil 2 cups of water and ½ cup of salt in a pan. Remove boiling mixture from the heat. Mix in 2 tablespoons of cooking oil, 2 tablespoons of alum*, and 2 cups of white flour. Return to medium heat and stir continuously until the liquid mixture forms a stiff ball with no gooey mixture left. Remove from the pan and allow cooling. While warm, knead the ball for 5 minutes.

*Alum prevents mold when dough is stored in the refrigerator. It is unnecessary if you use the dough within a day or two and allow your creations to air dry.

1. Tape the top of the cardboard tube so that the dough does not fall into it. Roll out the dough to about four inches wide, 10 inches long, and a bit thicker than ¼ inch. Lay the base of the cardboard tube at the bottom of the dough. Fold the top part over the cardboard or reed armature, leaving extra dough for the head. 2. Pinch the dough together down both sides. 3. Wrap the sides to the back to make a head. Once you have the form of a head, pinch the nose. You can put beads or small pebbles into the dough for eyes. 4. Stand up the finished figure so that it balances on the cardboard or reed armature. Allow to dry completely by letting it sit out in the air for a week. The dough will dry hard.

STUDENT GALLERY

This figure was made by Felicity.

1.  2.

3. 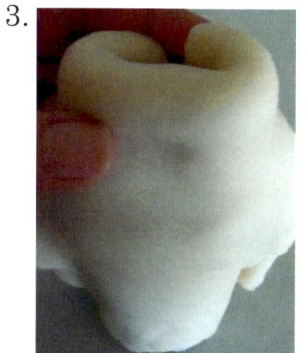 4.

Art in Palaces

Minoan Fresco Painting

The Minoans were adventurers, sailors, and traders who brought in food and other wealth from all the countries around them. They painted the more pleasant things of life. They painted in black, blue, rust, and golden brown colors, using beautiful black outlines to describe their subjects. Entertainers leaping over bulls, young boys boxing with gloves, or a man with a large catch of fish are some of the subjects for the paintings. They painted directly on the walls of their palaces, filling in the spaces with color.

Much of the artwork from Crete, a large island in the Mediterranean Sea, was discovered in fragments on the floors of ancient palaces. Some of the fragments were as tiny as the head of a pin (Marinatos). Restorers have carefully pieced the fragments together just as you would put together a puzzle. Many parts were missing and restorers had to fill in the missing portions. These portions appear smooth in reproductions of the artwork.

This lesson teaches us that the Minoan people decorated the walls and floors of their palaces with pictures of entertainers and the more pleasant activities people enjoyed.

Look at Fresco Painting
1500 B.C. Crete

In the painting below, a man leaps onto the back of a charging bull, while women are positioned on both sides. No one knows exactly how the leaping was done. People think that the three were trained entertainers and it is something like a circus act of today. This picture of a huge bull was painted onto a wall in a palace at Knossos, on the island of Crete. It was one of three palaces built by the Minoan civilization long ago. People now believe that the palace was the home of King Minos. In Greek literature, you can read about King Minos, his palace, and a magical maze that was home to a Minotaur. Bulls were a part of the Minoan peoples' stories and their art.

Is this bull standing still or does it seem to be running? How do you think the middle figure gets over the bull's horns and onto its back?

Do people use bulls for entertainment today? What kinds of stunts do rodeo cowboys do? What does a matador do?

Bull Jumping. Minoan fresco, 1500 BCE.
Location: Archaeological Museum, Heraklion, Crete, Greece
Photo Credit: Erich Lessing / Art Resource, NY

Project -You Make a Painting!

MATERIALS GROUP #2
Watercolor crayons
Watercolor paper
Brush
Black oil pastel (Group #1)

STUDENT GALLERY

This work is by Colleen (age 6). She uses a heavy black outline to show a horse, grass, and a border around the work.

The Minoans painted beautiful black outlines around the outside of their subjects. They also used black line to show fur, tails, eyes and other parts of the animal that they wanted to stand out. The illustration below shows the curvy lines used for the bull's fur.

You draw an animal or person using black line with a decorated border.

1. Draw a border two inches from the edge of the paper in black oil pastel.

2. Draw a pattern inside the border and draw the outline of an animal or person.

3. Add color using watercolor crayons. Once all areas are colored in, brush colored areas with water to blend the colors. The water-soluble paint will resist the black outline.

1.

2.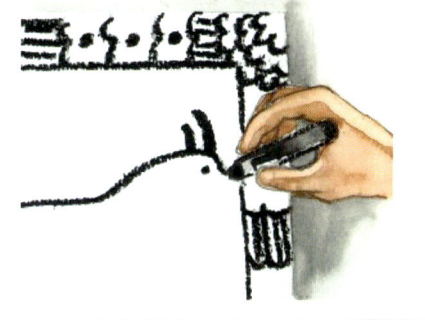

3.

Art in Pyramids

Egyptian Murals

Pyramids, tombs, and temples held Egyptian art. Large pyramids sealed the paintings from rain, wind, and sun, just like inside a cave. That is why we can still see them. Inside the pyramids, the walls were plastered. Plaster is a thick white paste that is still used on walls today. Once the plaster was dry, the walls were marked with a grid and artists began to draw the picture. They copied from small drawings carved into stones. To color the picture artists used blue, red, yellow and green pigments. Colored powders were mixed with beeswax or gum to make smooth paint. The paint was brushed on with frayed sticks from a palm tree or grass that was bundled together tightly. Sometimes a tomb was used before the paintings were completed. It was left unfinished and that is how we learned of the methods used by the Egyptians (Hayes).

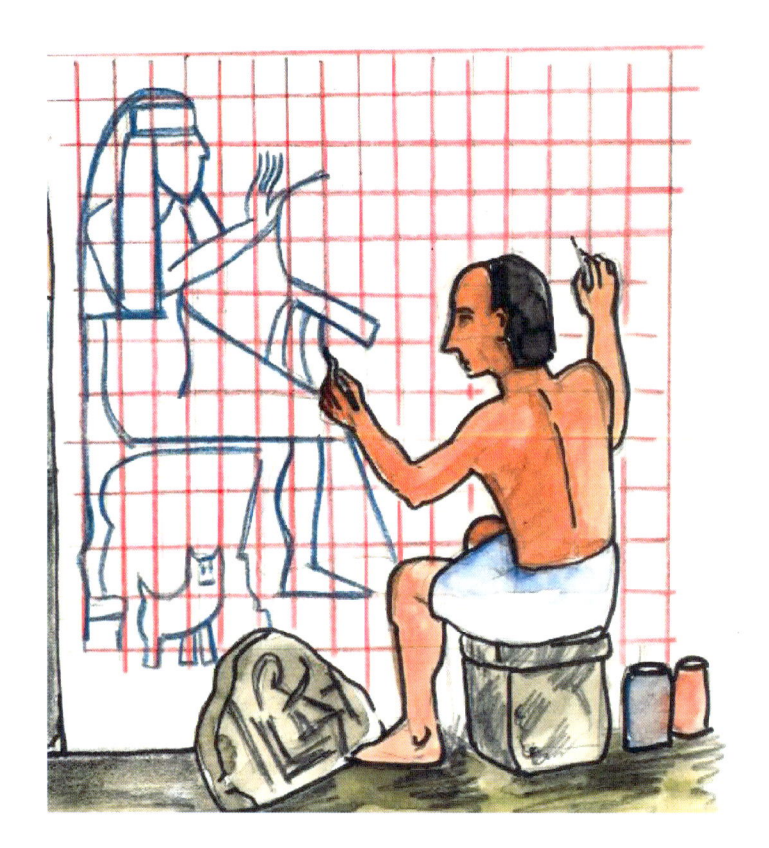

This lesson teaches us that Egyptian pharaohs built pyramids and decorated the interior walls with pictures that represented all activities of Egyptian life.

Look at Art in Pyramids
1400 B.C. Egypt

Scenes of everyday life filled Egyptian tombs within the pyramids. Bread making, ship building, harvesting, brick making, feasting and sports are some subjects found. They believed the scenes would come to life in the next world. Scenes showing every step of a harvest would supply them with plenty of provisions for their life after death. They often stacked one set of images above the other, as seen in the picture below. Egyptians read the pictures across as we would read words in a book. In this section of a wall painting, we see men harvesting grapes on the top row. In the second row men prepare the grapes and bottle the drink in large clay jugs. In the lower row we see an Egyptian boat used to transfer the beverage. Men wind ropes from reeds found at the edge of the Nile River. The round circles are bundles of ropes.

Harvesting and pressing grapes, making the most. Wall painting from the tomb of Kha-emwese. Egypt. Photo Credit: bpk, Berlin / Art Resource, NY Aegyptisches Museum, Staatliche Museen, Berlin, Germany

How do men carry grapes from the vineyard?

Can you find jars used for storing the beverage?

Where is the boat used for transporting goods? Where are the ropes that the men have wound? Four circles above their heads show their day's work.

Project -You Make a Mural!

A mural is a large picture usually painted directly onto a wall. Draw on a wall like the Egyptians.

1. Measure and tear off a sheet of paper from a roll. Tape the section to the wall at a height where you can reach it easily. Another option is to tip a table on its side and attach paper to that surface. Make sure that the table tips back slightly and is safe for children.

2. Use oil pastels to draw a picture of an activity you enjoy or that is a daily part of your life, just as the Egyptians did. Many students enjoy making people in Egyptian costume and other images from their Egyptian studies.

A small group of students can pretend to build a pyramid hallway. Set two tables on their sides against a wall or use three tables to form a U shaped hall. Announce to the crew that the Pharaoh has ordered a new hallway to be built within his great pyramid. Have a few students act out carving the hallway while others carry out the stones. Then, they plaster the wall (tape the paper onto the walls). Each student is assigned to a section of the wall to create the artwork with colored pastels. The children in the pictures below created their artwork in this way.

STUDENT GALLERY

This work is 3 feet tall and was completed by Bailey, (age 8). She chose to draw an Egyptian figure.

Art on Floors Egyptian Pavement Painting

Painted plaster floor scene of ducks and Nile plants from southern palace at Tell el-Amarna 18th dynasty 1353-1336 BC.
Photo Credit: Alfredo Dagli Orti / The Art Archive at Art Resource, NY Egyptian Museum Cairo

Pharaoh Akhenaten built the beautiful city of Akhetaten near the Nile River for himself and his queen in the 13th century B.C. The city included a palace for the queen, a temple for worship, a royal palace for the pharaoh, central quarters, and many luxurious homes along the edge of the river. Each home had its own flower garden, private lake, and pools. Pavilions opened to the lakes and provided shaded comfort in the open air. Among the many structures, floors were painted with nature scenes. Lotus bouquets, papyrus bunches with geese and ducks were painted on the smooth pavement that people walked on. Bright white walls were painted with men, animals, birds and fish that were seen along the Nile River. The ceilings were treated with hanging vines. Beautiful paintings adorned the residences of Egyptian royalty and high ranking officials from floor to ceiling. This is a picture of a portion of one pavement painting from the Maru-Aten Pavilion. This piece is now housed in the Egyptian museum in Cairo, Egypt.

How many different types of plants do you see in this section of the painting?
Look at the ducks. How does the artist show us that they are in flight? (by placing them above the plants and extending the wings outward)

Project -You Make a Floor Painting!

STUDENT GALLERY

Annalise (age 8) drew kangaroos, animals that would be seen in her area.

Draw a picture of birds or animals you might see if you took a trip to a water source like a pond, lake, or river. You can make a temporary drawing on smooth pavement using sidewalk chalk or a more permanent drawing on construction paper using soft pastels. You may even want to work on the floor instead of a table top so that you are creating a floor painting like the Egyptians.

When using soft pastels on paper you can cover a section with several colors laid down beside each other. Using your finger, a cotton ball, or tissue, you can blend the colors to create smooth areas.

In this work, the artist drew a bird that would be seen in his area. He used his finger to soften the edges of the leaves and the bird. The paper he worked on was large and a bit rough so that the pastel went on easily. A slick surfaced paper does not work when using chalk pastels.

When drawing on paper, have a parent seal the pastel with a light coat of hairspray when finished so that the drawing will not smear.

Art on City Walls

Near Eastern Bas-relief

A Bas-relief is a type of sculpture in where a carved image is raised above a background of solid stone. Bas-relief is pronounced (Baw- ree-leef), and is the same sound as our word, law.

Persian sculptors carved low reliefs in stone. The city of Persepolis was decorated with reliefs on walls and monuments to show the power of its rulers.

Great and mighty ancient civilizations arose in Mesopotamia, the land between the Tigris and Euphrates rivers. Because people needed to eat, they settled in places where they could grow crops. They dug canals, dams, and dikes to control the flow of water from the two rivers. Men built cities in areas where the water could be controlled and crops could be grown. Leaders became kings and kings took great pride in the cities they constructed and maintained. We do not know much about them because very few objects survived as one king conquered another and stole the treasures. What have survived are portions of walls that protected the cities. These walls were decorated with images of diplomats from conquered nations bringing gifts to the kings and images of kings as conquerors. Visitors and traders, entering the cities, had to pass along the walls and could clearly see the message that the images implied. The rulers were in charge and had great power.

Babylonian artists made walls and gates of glazed bricks. This detail was copied from the Gate of Ishtar, which included figures of bulls, dragons, and lions, which are all very powerful beasts.

> This lesson teaches us that walls surrounded the early cities of Mesopotamia. These walls were decorated with low-raised images called bas-reliefs.

Look at Bas-relief
883-859 B.C. City of Calah, Nineveh

The Assyrian city of Calah was surrounded by great walls. Pictures of men and lions were carved into the stone. These carved pictures were created to document stories of King Ashurnasirpal II's conquests. One of the oldest written stories from Mesopotamia told of the adventures of a powerful king, Gilgamesh, who fought an entire pride of lions and won. The story was popular throughout the ancient Middle East. Kings often showed themselves fighting lions, as Gilgamesh had done, and everyone remembered how powerful they were too. This scene shows a royal lion hunt. Men released the animals from cages into an area surrounded by men with shields. Here the king participates in the hunt while a great lion attacks the royal chariot from behind. The king rises above the lion ready to release the arrow. This scene spoke to all about the king's courage and ability to dominate his enemies no matter how powerful.

How many horses are shown in this section of the wall? How many lions are shown in this section of the wall?

Where are the men with shields? Where is the chariot driver?

Look closely at the decoration on the horses and the chariot. These decorations identify it as the king's chariot. Which man is King Ashurnasirpal II?

Does the king show his power in this scene by standing above or below the lion?

Stone panel from the North-West Palace of Ashurnasirpal II, (Room B, Panel 19), Nimrud (ancient Kalhu), northern Iraq, Neo-Assyrian, 883-859 BC. This alabaster relief shows the royal sport of kings. Royal lion hunts were a very old tradition in Mesopotamia, with examples of similar scenes known as early as 3000 BC. King Ashumasirpal obviously took great pleasure from the activity as he claims in inscriptions to have killed a total of 450 lions. The motif of King Ashurnasirpa III or the crown prince hunting.
Location: British Museum, London, Great Britain. Photo Credit: HIP / Art Resource, NY.

Project -You Make a Bas-relief!

The figures in the lion hunt from the previous page rise out of the background. You can make a bas-relief too. You will work with clay.

STUDENT GALLERY

Connor (age 6) made a bas-relief of his dog. It was painted with tempera paints after the clay dried.

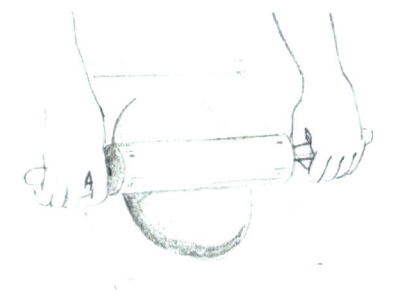

1. Work on a sheet of foil or wax paper, taped to the tabletop. Roll a ball of clay flat with a rolling pin, just as you would roll out sugar cookies. Roll to a depth between 1/2 to 3/8 inches in thickness. A thicker slab is better than a thin slab so that you do not press all the way through the clay.

2. Carve an outline of a figure into the slab with a toothpick, pencil, large nail, or any object with a point.

3. Push clay away from the main form with a clay tool or kitchen utensil. Fingers may also be used to make the main figure rise from the background.

4. Add textures by pressing into the clay with your fingers, the end of a pencil, or any tool you find around the house. All tools can be cleaned with water. If you want to hang the bas-relief, press two holes all the way through the clay near the top, using a pencil. Allow the bas-relief to dry for a few days. Loop a string through the holes and hang.

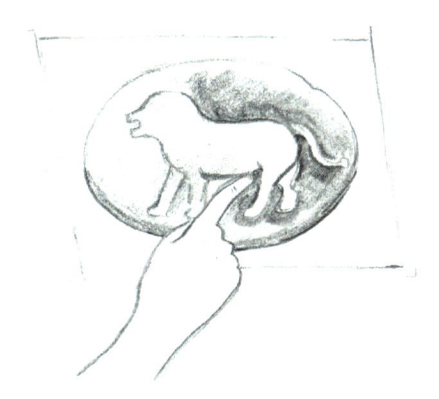

Art on Pots

Greek Pottery

The people who settled in Greece built great cities. They wrote poetry and developed new ways of governing the people. They painted pictures on walls, carved statues, and decorated pottery. Their art developed into a realistic style that influenced the art of Rome and later, the art of the Renaissance. Only a few fragments of the paintings survived, but we can see some statues and many types of pottery.

The earliest Greek pottery was painted with geometric designs, but by 800 B.C. animal and human figures were put into the decoration. Vase painters painted unique scenes on every pot. Greek vase painters focused on the people of Greece and their activities as subjects for their art. They painted people doing many of the same types of things that we enjoy today. Women are shown in groups playing music. Men are involved in physical sports, table games, and horseback riding. Pots even show artists painting pots. Since the Greeks lived by the Mediterranean Sea, they were fond of drawing men in ships. They also enjoyed the stories compiled by Homer. These were stories of the Greek gods and heroes that they worshiped and honored. Many scenes from these stories are found on pottery.

This lesson teaches us that the art of Greece is about its people. Pictures of people and their activities are found on the many pots they made.

Look at Art on Pots
400 B.C. Greece

Painting from Greece survives through their pottery. They painted on clay, usually with black paint, or white as shown below. This image is painted inside a cup. A warrior attacks. While the title calls the creature a dragon, it looks more like a snake because it has no legs.

How many birds do you see? Can you find the rabbit hiding among the flowers? How many flowers are shown?

Point out the creatures that are a threat to the birds.

Greek architecture (buildings) had pillars. Can you find a pillar?

What image is seen on the warrior's shield?

Painter of Horsemen (6th BCE), Cadmos killing the dragon of Thebes or Apollo and the serpent Python. Laconian cup, c. 550 -540 BCE. From Caere, laconian style III. Diam. 18.5 cm. inv.: E 669. Photo: Hervé Lewandowski. Location: Louvre, Paris, France. Photo Credit: Réunion des Musées Nationaux / Art Resource, NY

Project - You Make a Pinch Pot!

Make a pot. Paint a picture or design on the pot like the Greeks. Take out as much self-hardening clay as needed and reseal the rest in the bag. You will have about an hour to work with the clay before it begins to dry and harden. It will dry completely in a few days and can then be painted.

STUDENT GALLERY

Your pot can be made with red or gray clay. You may want to use white watercolor crayon as well as black. This pot featuring a warrior shooting a flaming arrow is by John (age 6).

1. Form a ball of clay in the palm of your hand. Roll the ball in all directions on a tabletop until it is smooth and round.

2. Press your thumb into the center and turn the pot while squeezing into the sides with your thumb and fingers until a bowl shape is formed.

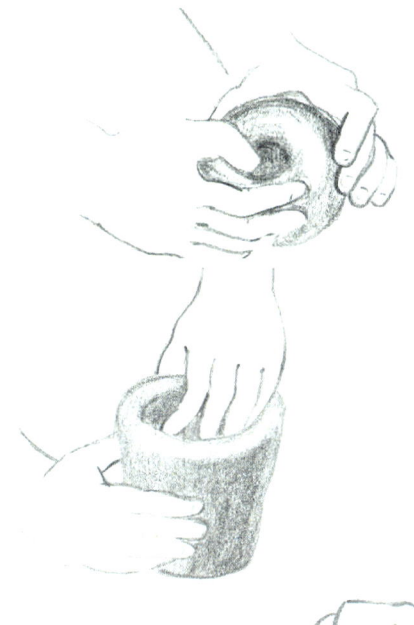

3. Squeeze the sides of the pot until it is the right shape, but leave the sides at least ¼ inch thick. When the pot is the right shape, dip your finger into a small can of water and rub the entire surface gently to make it smooth. Allow the pot to dry for two to three days.

4. To paint the pot, dip the tip of a black watercolor crayon into a can of water. Adults may want to only put a half inch of water into the can so that students cannot get the crayon too wet. Paint a design or picture onto the pot, dipping the crayon tip into water as needed. Let dry.

WATER

Art in Tombs

Etruscan Wall Painting

The Etruscan people lived very close to the Greeks. They were the earliest known inhabitants of Italy. What we know about them comes from underground rooms that are a lot like basements. In these rooms, called tombs, they buried the dead. Only rich men and women could afford to have their tomb painted with pictures. The pictures tell us about Etruscan people. Some items found in the rooms include small, decorated mirrors, with phrases written on them. By this, we know that women as well as men were educated and could read. Etruscan women enjoyed some of the freedoms and rights that women in America and Europe are accustomed to today. One of these freedoms was that they ate at the table with men. It was not so in all ancient societies including Greece and Rome. We see men and women dining and dancing together in the pictures on Etruscan tomb walls.

> This lesson teaches us that Etruscan art is found in the tombs of wealthy people.

Look at Wall Painting
320-310 B.C. Etruscan from Italy

This flute player is part of an interior wall painting by the Etruscan people. Etruscans often painted people in natural settings doing things that were common in their culture like hunting birds, mounting a chariot, lounging at a banquet table, or dancing as musicians play. They are dressed in the traditional loosely draped clothing worn by the Greeks and later the Romans. The Etruscans made paint from common elements around them. White was made from chalk. Black was made from charcoal. Red came from rust. Blue was a mixture of copper, calcium, and silica.

What kind of shoes does this Etruscan musician wear?

What kind of instrument does he play?

What kinds of marks does the artist use to paint the plants? (lines, dots, etc.)

How did the artist paint ground? (a wide line)

Does the artist show us what is behind the musician?

In this painting, the artist was only interested in painting the musician and what was near him.

Flutist entertaining the banqueters. Tomb of the Leopards, Tarqinia, 480-470BCE. Etruscan wall painting. Early 5th BCE. Location: Tomb of the Leopards, Tarquinia, Italy
Photo Credit: Scala / Art Resource, NY

Project -You Make a Silhouette!

STUDENT GALLERY

This student work is by Kay, (age 6).

Etruscans, like the Egyptians, painted faces from the side. A side view is called a silhouette. You can color a picture of yourself from the side. You will need a partner to help you draw the outline.

1. Have an adult set up a light that shines at a wall. Tape a piece of paper on the wall.

2. Sit facing sideways so that a shadow of your face projects onto the paper. Get as close to the wall as possible to make a sharper shadow image. A partner then draws around the outside edge of the shadow that is seen on the paper.

3. Color in the silhouette using oil pastels. Fill in all the spaces and put colors over other colors to mix them. Choose pastels that most closely match your hair, eye, and skin color. Add details like hats or bows.

If you had fun with this project, you may want to make a drawing of your whole body. You will need a roll of paper at least 24 to 36 inches wide. Roll it out onto the floor. Lay on your back, onto the paper, with your arms in the pose that you want. A helper can trace around your body. Next, turn your head to the side and copy around your head, lining up the neck to the body. This is always the way the Etruscan's drew heads. Draw over the outlines with dark  oil pastel. Now fill in the entire body with the clothing you want. Add birds, trees, or other objects around the figure. This could be a project that you come back to repeatedly. Have fun!

Art in Streets

Roman Sculpture

In Roman cities, one could find art in the streets. Sculptors used stone and bronze (a shiny metal). The statues were often life size or larger. Romans used art in their streets to remind people of their power. Each day as Roman citizens and slaves passed the sculptures, they remembered who was in control of their lives. These statues were usually of gods, goddesses, emperors and great generals. Statues decorated large public buildings like coliseums and amphitheaters where people went to watch spectacular shows.

Entertainments such as sports and theatre were violent and resulted in many deaths among those participating. Art in Roman homes was of a more pleasant nature showing birds, pet dogs, bowls of fruit, and other domestic subjects of the time.

This lesson teaches us that Romans used art in the streets to show the power of the emperor or general and as a way of reminding the people who was in control.

76

Look at Sculpture
2nd Century Rome

This sculpture was built to show the emperor's power over his enemies. Emperor Marcus Aurelius was a hater and persecutor of the Christian faith. Those accused of being Christian could be captured and taken to a coliseum. There they would be forced to participate in a sport, which would result in their deaths. It was a difficult time to be a Christian.

It was said that Aurelius had such power over his enemies that he had only to extend his hand to make them lay down their weapons. Here his right arm is extended. There was originally a fallen figure under the horse's raised leg to remind people of this message. This sculpture stood in a second century Roman street (Ambra).

Does the horse look strong?

Do you think a person could walk around this statue to see it from all sides?

How would you feel standing below the emperor, looking into his eyes as shown here?

Emperor Marcus Aurelius (161-180 CE).
Equestrian statue, originally gilded bronze from the Capitol Square,
Location: Rome, Italy
Photo Credit: Erich Lessing / Art Resource, NY

Project -You Sculpt!

STUDENT GALLERY

This horse was formed by Audrey (age 7).

You can make a small animal sculpture in clay. The sculpture is made by pulling forms out from the center rather than adding parts to it. Pieces added on will fall off when the form dries. By pulling parts out, the form is made of the same piece and is strong.

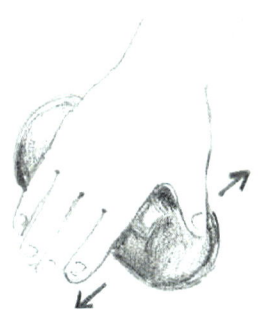

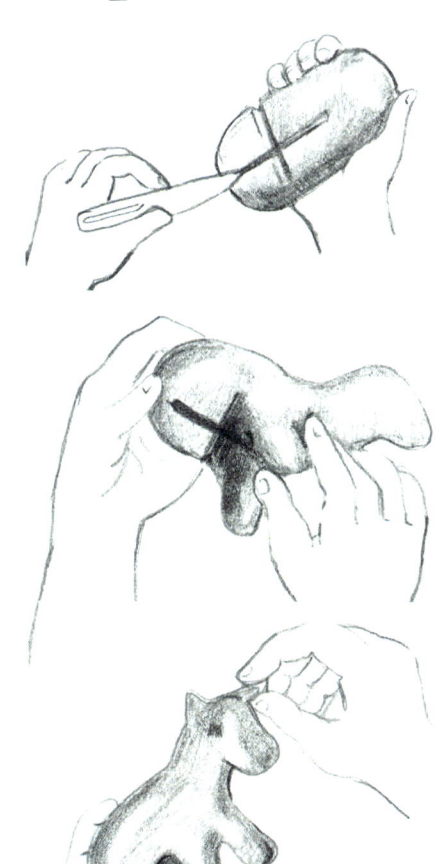

1. Form a ball from clay. Roll the ball into a cylinder using a back and forth motion between the palm of your hand and the table surface. Keep it thick. All parts of the animal will be pulled from this one piece.

2. Save one end for the neck and head. Cut a cross on the other end with a plastic knife.

3. Pull out the **large** forms like the head and neck. Pull the legs out from each section of the cross. Keep the neck and legs thick and sturdy, shaping as necessary. Do not add pieces on.

4. Pull out the **small** forms like ears and tail. Do not make any thin pieces. Keep them thick so that they will not break off after the clay has dried.

5. Let the clay sculpture dry for 2-4 days. The clay can be painted with tempera paint.

Art on Roadsides Roman Portraits

All ancient civilizations painted and formed figures to represent people, but they rarely added the specific details needed to show whom each figure was. The Romans employed Greek artists to make portraits carved into stone, showing unique features so that all could recognize whom the person was. The busts (showing head to chest) of emperors, generals, philosophers, orators, and athletes could be seen in villas (private homes) everywhere. By displaying busts of important people, Romans were telling others that they were well educated.

Romans conquered many nations and took slaves, but they allowed slaves to become free if they would become supporters of any plebeian (the people in power). Children of the "freemen" were free of all special restrictions and were true Roman citizens. To help freemen to be proud of their special place in Roman society, plebeians offered to have monuments placed along roads outside the city to honor the freemen. A monument was a carved relief in stone or marble and showed portraits of the freeman with his sons or his wife. The people were framed as if they were looking out a window.

This carved statue is of a stone-cutter. A stone-cutter cut stones just like this one for Roman citizens. See the wedge and chisel in his hand. These are the tools he worked with. His profession became a part of his tomb stone.

Stone-cutter. Detail of a funeral stele from Vicentrue (Necropolis) on the road to Reims.
Location:
Musee d'Art et d'Histoire, Metz, France
Photo Credit:
Erich Lessing / Art Resource, NY

Project -You Model a Portrait!

MATERIALS GROUP #4
Self-hardening clay
Plastic knife, rolling pin or dowel

STUDENT GALLERY

This relief portrait was made from clay and sculpted by Nathanael (age 7).

You model a portrait from clay. Slice off two pieces of clay ½ inch thick. With one piece, roll a slab for the background. With the other, slice out a circle with a pencil or pointed stick. (1.) Scratch lines into the back of the circle and the slab then press the pieces together firmly. (2.) Smooth the edges with fingers. Use your fingers to squeeze a nose and to push in the eye sockets. Pull up the nose with a squeeze. (3.) Roll balls of clay and press onto sockets. Smash two more balls and cut the flattened circle in half. Use these as eye lids on top and bottom of each eye. (4.) Make balls for hair. Score each ball and the place on the head where you want to place it before pressing them together. Roll small cylinders to form the lips. Press these pieces onto the face. Smooth all edges by pressing with fingers. Set the portrait on a piece of paper and allow it to dry for several days.

1.

2.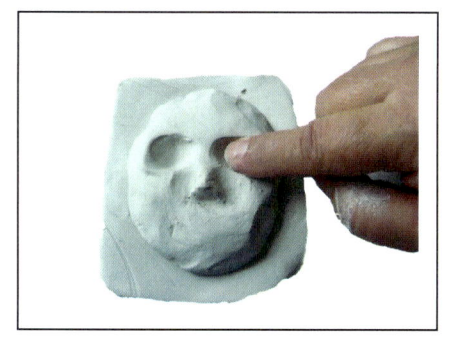

3.

4.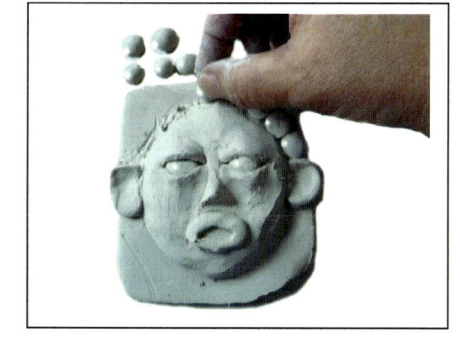

Art in Churches

Byzantine Mosaics

On the walls and domes of early churches, one could find pictures made from tiny pieces of glass, pottery, jewels, precious metals, or stone. These dark churches were lit by candlelight. Pieces of colored glass caught the flickering light of candles and glimmered or sparkled. Sheets of gold were attached to clear glass and placed in the wall at angles so that light reflected off the gold areas and sparkled as one walked around the room. This gave an almost heavenly appearance to the pictures. This type of picture, called a mosaic, is like a jigsaw puzzle with pieces fitting tightly together. When the first churches came into existence in Roman territory, they were decorated using mosaics just as the Romans had done in their homes and public buildings.

This lesson teaches us that mosaics were used in the first Christian churches to show the subjects in a heavenly glow as the candles flickered onto the gold and jewels that were embedded into plaster.

Look at Mosaics
7th Century in Italy

Mosaic art is made by arranging small pieces of colored glass or stone onto a wall or floor. The art of making mosaics dates back to Mesopotamia. The Romans used mosaics on floors and on walls. Byzantine art incorporated Roman tastes. In the Byzantine period, which followed the fall of Rome, this elaborate method of creating art was perfected. It could now be used on the high walls and ceilings in the newly constructed churches. Byzantine art is a mixture of Christian images and non-Christian ones. This is a mosaic of an angel that was made on a domed ceiling.

Can you see the small pieces that make up the picture?

Look at the pattern on the angel wings. Do the wing patterns look like a peacock's wings?

How many colors of tile do you see in the angel's robe? Where do you see gold tiles?

The Archangel Gabriel, 7th Century. Photo Credit: Dover Publications Inc., NY.

Project -You Make a Mosaic!

Make a mosaic using colored paper instead of bits of glass and stone. If you find you like this kind of art, you can get real mosaic tiles and other materials at art supply stores. To make your mosaic follow these steps:

STUDENT GALLERY

This artwork is by Linsey (age 10).

1.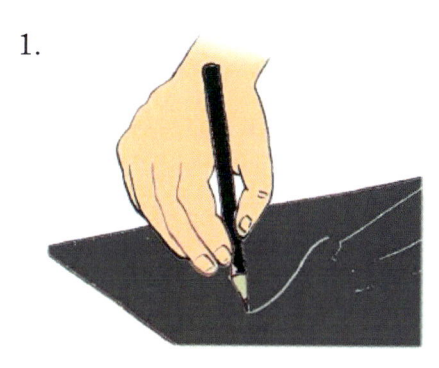

2.

3.

1. On black paper, draw outlines of the objects in the picture. Draw the lines so that you can see where to put the paper pieces. Make the objects large enough so pieces of paper fit into them.

2. Cut brightly colored paper into small pieces. Use colors that you want to put into the mosaic. Bright colors look best on a black background. Larger, one inch pieces, on a black sheet about 12"x17" are easier for young ones to work with. You can glue two sheets of black paper together to make one large sheet.

3. Using a glue stick, press the glue onto one piece at a time. Press the squares of paper onto the black paper. Continue in this way until the spaces are filled up.

Art in Castles

Medieval Tapestry

The Middle Ages was the time of knights, castles, and princesses. However, life for people in Europe was far from a fairytale with a happy ending. Wars lasted year after year and soon people only had time to get food and protect themselves. There was little time to do fun things like participate in sports or make art. Cities and towns became ruins. People turned to farming and relied on a lord (wealthy landowner), who protected them by allowing them to live within his castle walls. Women rarely left the protection of the castle. They prepared food and made clothing. Women probably made all the tapestries for the castle. The tapestry shown on the next page is a rare object, because of its large size, and because it tells a story that actually took place. It tells the story in pictures, relying on few words. Because castles were big with areas open to the outside, tapestries and rugs were used to keep out the cold. These were decorated with art.

> This lesson teaches us that art in castles was rare, but an embroidered cloth was made to tell about a historic event. It is called the *Bayeux Tapestry.*

Look at Medieval Embroidery
1070-1080 Canterbury, England

Imagine women, protected by castle walls, sewing a record of history. This art is not a painting but an embroidered cloth that stretches over 230 feet in length. That is nearly as long as a football field. Into this huge length of fabric is stitched the events that happened in 1065-1066 leading up to the Norman Conquest of England. It is a mixture of pictures and words written in Latin. We do not know where or how it hung or if it was rolled up like a scroll and stored as a record for William the Conqueror's defeat of the English King Harold. A small section of the embroidered scroll is shown below. This tapestry has a center strip in which the main action takes place. A top and lower strip show those fallen in battle, fallen in quicksand, men plowing and sowing seed, men loading the boats, dogs, griffins, lions, dragons, birds, fish, eels, and other creatures encountered on the journey. For a look at much of the tapestry see "900 Years Ago: The Norman Conquest" by Kenneth M. Setton, PH.D. Litt.D.

What animals do you see in the lower strip of this section?

How many people are in the center boat? How many horses do they travel with? How many men use oars on each boat?

Why do you think some boats are smaller than others are? How did the artists show water?

Anonymous, 11th century. The Norman fleet sets sail for England. Bayeux Tapestry, embroidery.
Location: Musee de la Tapisserie, Bayeux, France
Photo Credit: Erich Lessing / Art Resource, NY

Project - You Make Cloth Art!

What is happening in the world around you? What recent historical events have taken place? These events might be within your own family. Have you taken a trip, moved into a new home, or celebrated a birthday? Draw a picture on cloth to tell a story so that the event can be remembered.

This ship is by Antoine (age 9).

1. Tape the edges of a small, pre-washed piece of cotton cloth to a flat surface using masking tape. White cloth works best. Draw a picture on it using oil pastels.

Note: When students have finished the artwork, place a piece of paper over and under the cloth artwork and iron it lightly with a warm iron. The paper absorbs extra color and the heat sets the pastels giving the image a nice shine.

2. If you know an adult who sews, you may ask for help with adding a colorful fabric frame around the edges of the cloth picture. Roll up the cloth like a scroll and tie with a ribbon to store your picture.

Embroidery is made on a piece of cloth. Fancy stitches sewn into the cloth make lines and fill in spaces. If you are interested in doing a real embroidery check out the book, *My First Embroidery Book, A Name Sampler,* by Winky Cherry. Her second editions were published in 2011.

Art in Windows

Gothic Glass

Castles, knights on horseback, peasants, kings, and great church cathedrals were all a part of living in the Middle Ages. These people had never seen a TV or movie screen where colorful images are projected with light. When they looked at stained-glass windows, it was a glorious sight. People thought it was like viewing an image of heaven as sunlight streamed through bits of colored glass. Sparkling streams of colored light flooded into the dark church space. The church was a major part of each person's life in the Middle Ages. At a time when there were few freedoms, the church was the one place that everyone could enter – from the poorest peasants to the wealthiest lords and kings.

To make stained-glass windows, glassmakers mixed ashes from burnt wood and clean sand. They then melted the mixture at high temperatures. Metals were added to the hot mixture for color. They scooped up a ball of liquid glass on the end of a hollow pipe, like a straw, and blew into it until it formed a bubble. They cut the end off the bubble.

Quickly swirling the bubble, it would flatten into a large circle. After it cooled, the glasscutters cut it into shapes that they had drawn onto a wooden surface. Surfaces were painted in black and then fired in a kiln (oven) to fuse the paint to the glass. Finished glass pieces were joined with strips of lead using a hot grozing iron (Macaulay).

This lesson teaches us that colorful glass windows were an important part of the medieval person's spiritual experience. The effect relied on sunlight to shine through the glass, throwing sparkling streams of color throughout the church, reminding people that God is light.

Look at Stained Glass Windows
13th Century France

Chartres: Stained-glass rose window. Gothic.
Location: Cathedral, Chartres, France
Photo Credit: Vanni / Art Resource, NY

King David with Harp. Detail of Lancet Window. North Transept, Catherdral, Chartres.

It may be hard to imagine making art with sunlight but that is what people did over one thousand years ago. Abbot Surger dreamed of a church building that reminded people of God as they entered it. The new church had tall pointed towers like fire to remind people that God was warmth. Light, let in through huge windows, was to remind people that God was light. The windows were made of colored glass that was cut into shapes to make a picture. The Christian faith was told in these pictures. It was a bright storybook that everyone could read.

Kings are honored in windows below the circle. King David is shown in the close-up and in the second window from the left. What instrument is he playing?

For a look at more stained glass windows see the following article: MacLeish, "Chartes: Legacy from the Age of Faith", National Geographic Society, December 1969.

Project-You Make Colored Windows!

Make a type of stained glass window using colorful tissue paper for the glass and black paper to hold the work together. When taped to a window the light shines through the tissue paper just like colored glass!

STUDENT GALLERY

This work is by Callista (age 7).

1. Fold a piece of paper in half then in half again. You may use any color, but black makes the bright colored tissue paper stand out best.

You will have two folded sides.

2. Cut shapes through all four layers. Cut on the two folded sides to make shapes on the inside of the final piece. Cut shapes on the unfolded sides to make shapes on the outside edges of the final piece.

3. Cut pieces of tissue paper large enough to fit over each cut shape. Glue around each cut shape on the backside of the black paper. Press the tissue paper onto the glued edges. Fill each cut shape with colorful tissue paper. When finished turn it over and hang it in a window.

Art in Books

Medieval Illumination

If you wanted to tell a story in the Middle Ages, you would probably speak it, rather than read it from a book. In those days, books with pictures were not common like they are today because they took a long time to make. Monks, men who devoted their lives to God and who were protected by the walls of the church, wrote books by hand. They were trained in fancy writing called calligraphy and picture making. The pictures are called illuminations because they brightened or lit up the page. To make the pages monks used quill pens, colored paint, and often added real gold and silver to the pages. They decorated them with elaborate figures, animals, letters, and designs.

This lesson teaches us that monks, in churches during the Middle Ages, practiced book illumination. The pages of the books were brightly decorated with words and pictures.

Look at Illumination
13th Century, North Midlands, England

One type of illumination popular in the 12th and 13th centuries in England and France is the Bestiary. This type of book describes a variety of animals and birds. The pictures show rocks and plants as well. The illustrations were accompanied by a moral lesson. Often beasts had symbolic meanings that explained ideas like good and evil. This piece of art is a picture from a page of a Bestiary.

The page is split into three sections. The top section shows a male lion. What does the lion see on his journey?

What is shown in the middle section?

How many cubs do you see in the middle section?

What do you think the red area represents? Could it be a cave or grassy nest?

Both male and female lions are in the bottom section. How many cubs do you see? Look at the color of each to see which cubs are male and which are female.

Do you think this page is a type of story line and the cubs have left their nest in the bottom section and enter the landscape that their father roamed in the top section?

How would you tell the story from top to bottom?

English Bestiary, 1210. North Midlands England Three illustrations of lions from an early 13th-century English Bestiary. Photo Credit Dover Publications Inc. NY

Project -You Make a Book!

MATERIALS GROUP #2
Paper
Watercolor crayons

You illustrate a book about animals like in a Bestiary. Start by thinking up a story. You may want to tell a story. You can write it down, dictate the words to an adult as they write it down, or tell the story entirely in pictures.

A story has these four parts: MAIN CHARACTER, SETTING, PROBLEM, SOLVING THE PROBLEM (Resolution).

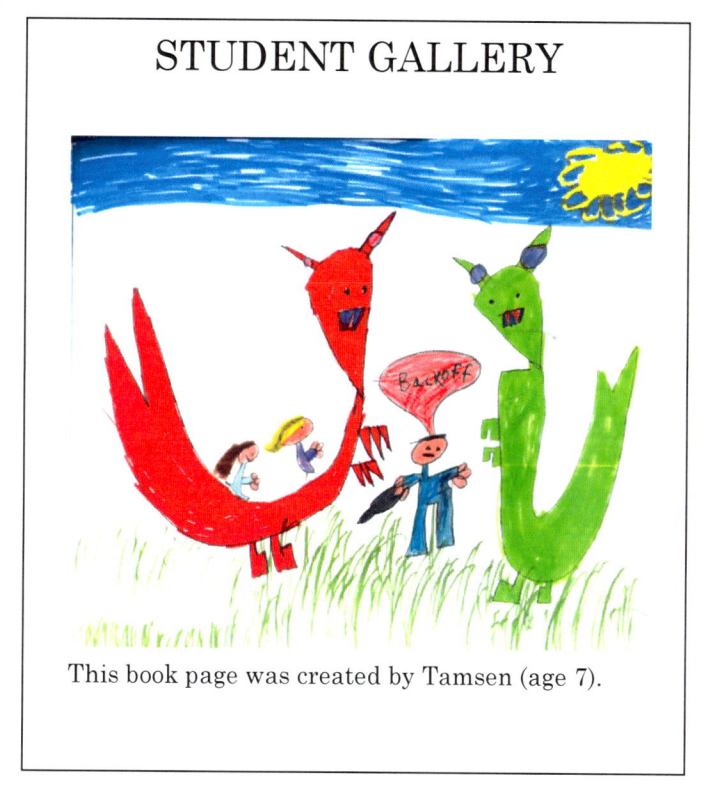

STUDENT GALLERY

This book page was created by Tamsen (age 7).

1. The main character is who the story is about. Your main character can be a person like you, an animal, insect, a machine that thinks, or someone you imagine.

2. The setting is where the story takes place. The story can take place in a small area such as on a leaf or in a pond. It can take place in a certain city or country. It can even take place in outer space or a period like the Middle Ages when knights roamed the countryside.

3. In every story you will find that the main character has a problem. The character may try to solve the problem several times without success. Problems can be common experiences like being hungry, being lost, or having a dog that won't stay home.

4. The final part of the story happens when the main character solves the problem. Try thinking of several ways the main character could do this. Choose the one you like best. Once you know your story, start making the pages.

Adults organize the pages with numbers and keep them in order within a folder. You may want to read *The Very Hungry Caterpillar* by Eric Carle. Have students identify the four parts of this simple story.

Art on Book Covers Medieval Scriptoria

Education and learning were not practiced in many places within Europe during the early Middle Ages. Libraries had closed and been destroyed. Christian monasteries helped preserve manuscripts of religious works from the Bible, and writings from ancient Greece and Rome. Monks, working in monasteries, copied and produced many manuscripts in special workshops called *scriptoria*. The covers for Medieval manuscripts were highly decorated to show that the book inside was important. Covers were made of leather or wood with painted decoration. Many include jewels, ivory carvings, and other elaborate ornamentation. Some covers were woven or decorated with pictures using colored thread. Every part of the book was made by hand. This laborious work helped preserve the writings of ancient times so that we have them to read today. Private libraries and places of learning did not emerge again until the 1300's and 1400's during a time we call the Renaissance.

How many jewels are used on this book cover?

Can you find the lion on a pedestal? The lion is a symbol for the Apostle Mark.

Can you find the head of a bull on a pedestal? The bull is a symbol for Luke.

Where is the head of an eagle? The eagle is a symbol for the evangelist John.

Can you find the head of a man on a pedestal? The man represents Matthew.

What two figures are in the center of the cover?

Original front cover of a Missal with Virgin and Child, Evangelists and Saints. Silver gilt and jeweled plaque. Germany (Abbey of Weingarten), c.1200-1232.MS. M.710, front cover.
Location: The Pierpont Morgan Library, New York, NY, U.S.A.
Photo Credit: The Pierpont Morgan Library / Art Resource, NY

Project –You Make a Cover

MATERIALS GROUP #3
Construction paper
Scissors
Additional binding materials
Optional: gold paper, plastic jewels,
glue

Once you have completed the inside pages
from the previous lesson, make front and
back covers for your book. Cut two pieces of
colored card stock or construction paper to
the size of the pages. Decorate the cover by
cutting out shapes. Glue the shapes onto the
cover paper. Organize the book pages like
this:

STUDENT GALLERY

You can add gold paper and plastic jewels to the
cover of your book. Grace (age 5) cut out gold
paper to make a castle, stars, and crowns.

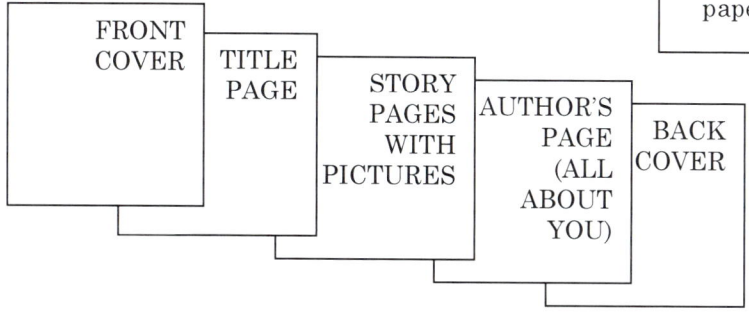

FRONT COVER — TITLE PAGE — STORY PAGES WITH PICTURES — AUTHOR'S PAGE (ALL ABOUT YOU) — BACK COVER

Use one of the following binding techniques for your
book.

STAPLE
Stack all pages neatly. Use paper clips to secure the
pages. Staple through all the pages along the left edge.
This technique works well for ten pages or less.

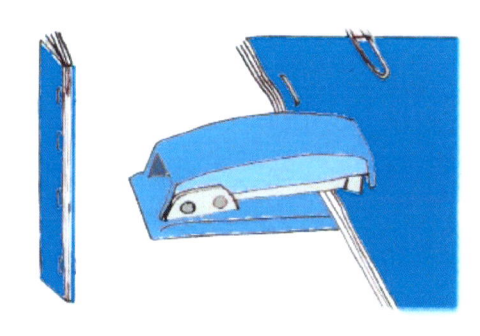

PUNCH AND TIE
Stack all pages neatly. Use paper clips to secure pages.
Mark where you want the holes along the left edge.
Punch holes. Tie loops with string, ribbon or yarn.

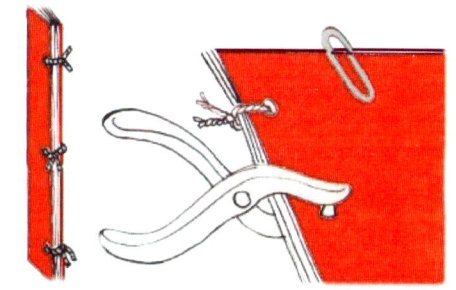

SEW
An adult can punch holes along the left edge by
hammering with an awl or a nail through all the pages.
A drill can also be used. The student uses a long
shoestring to sew. Tie a knot at one end of the book, sew
in and out then tie a knot at the other end. Note: The tip
of a piece of yarn or string can be dipped into liquid glue
and dried. This keeps the ends from fraying.

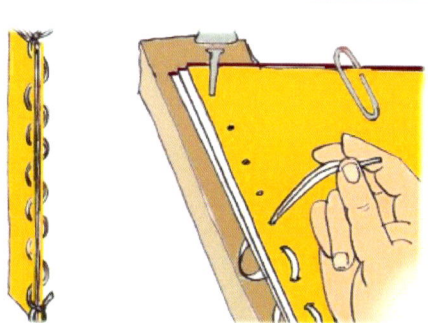

Bibliography

Carle, Eric *The Very Hungry Caterpillar*, Philomel Books, 1986.

Casteret, Norbert "Lascaux Cave: Cradle of World Art," National Geographic Society, Dec. 1948.

Cherry, Winky *My First Embroidery Book,* Palmer-Pletsch Associates, 2011.

E'Ambra, Eve "Art and Identity in the Roman World," The Everyman Art Library, Copyright 1998.

Hayes, William C. "Daily Life in Ancient Egypt", National Geographic Society, October 1941.

Judge, Joseph "Minoans and Mycenaeans: Greece's Brilliant Bronze Age," National Geographic Society, February 1978.

Macaulay, David, *Cathedral, The Story of Its Construction,* The Trumpet Club, 1973.

MacLeish, "Chartes: Legacy from the Age of Faith", National Geographic Society, December 1969.

Marinatos, Spyridon "Thera, Key to the Riddles of Minos," National Geographic Society, May 1972.

Rigaud, Jean – Philippe "Art Treasures from the Ice Age: Lascaux Cave," National Geographic Society, Oct. 1988.

Setton, Ph. D., Litt. D., Kenneth M., "900 Years Ago: The Norman Conquest", National Geographic Society, August 1966.

Art History
Projects Encouraging Creativity

Artistic Pursuits Early Elementary, K-3, Book One - An Introduction to the Visual Arts is sure to delight young students with colorful illustrations and great Masters' paintings and prints. The THIRD EDITION features more Master works, more demonstrated technique, and more lessons. 36 lessons complete a one year course and capture your child's interests and imagination while introducing fundamental principles of the visual arts.

"Thx again for a program my kids ASK to do!! "

Homeschool Parent - Lynda Reid / South Africa

"I just wanted to tell you how much I LOVE this curriculum! I have been searching high and low for an art curriculum that actually teaches art (not glorified cut and paste or copy the adult model) at an affordable price, and that is easy to use. I have found what I was looking for and so much more! Not only does your curriculum actually teach art (real art!) at the child's level, we get art history and art appreciation too!"

Homeschool Parent – Carey Clapp / Wyoming

"The instruction is so well-suited to the book's audience of kindergarten to 3rd graders. Mrs. Ellis uses a conversational style of writing that is so appealing to younger children, yet her curriculum never "talks down" to them (nor does it go over their heads!)

Homeschool Parent – Jenny Thompson / Florida

'I'm not exaggerating in the least when I say that from the first project, the whole family was hooked...we love this curriculum. It's the whole package in one easy simple to teach format."

Homeschool Parent – Laurie Gauger / Illinois

**Published by
Artistic Pursuits Inc.
www.artisticpursuits.com**

Non-consumable
Use this book again and again!

Early Elementary K-3 Book One   USA

$47.95
ISBN 978-1-939394-01-9

54795>

9 781939 394019

This book has shown thousands of young students how to create original works of art while laying a solid educational foundation under their feet. Your role as parent/teacher is to read the text, discuss ideas and then let students explore the possibilities. Add to that your praise and encouragement. You and your students will love it! Start today.